T0329106

# Cambridge Elements ☰

**Elements in American Politics**
edited by
**Frances Lee**
*University of Maryland*

# LEGISLATIVE HARDBALL

*The House Freedom Caucus and the
Power of Threat-Making in
Congress*

Matthew N. Green
*The Catholic University of America*

CAMBRIDGE
UNIVERSITY PRESS

# CAMBRIDGE
## UNIVERSITY PRESS

University Printing House, Cambridge CB2 8BS, United Kingdom

One Liberty Plaza, 20th Floor, New York, NY 10006, USA

477 Williamstown Road, Port Melbourne, VIC 3207, Australia

314–321, 3rd Floor, Plot 3, Splendor Forum, Jasola District Centre,
New Delhi – 110025, India

79 Anson Road, #06–04/06, Singapore 079906

Cambridge University Press is part of the University of Cambridge.

It furthers the University's mission by disseminating knowledge in the pursuit of
education, learning, and research at the highest international levels of excellence.

www.cambridge.org
Information on this title: www.cambridge.org/9781108735810
DOI: 10.1017/9781108677011

© Matthew Green 2019

First published 2019

*A catalogue record for this publication is available from the British Library.*

ISBN 978-1-108-73581-0 Paperback
ISBN 9781108677011 Online
ISSN 2515-1592 print
ISSN 2515-1606 online

# Legislative Hardball

## The House Freedom Caucus and the Power of Threat-Making in Congress

Elements in American Politics

DOI: 10.1017/9781108677011
First published online: February 2019

Matthew N. Green
*The Catholic University of America*

**Abstract:** Assertive bargaining occurs from time to time in the U.S. Congress. It became an important feature of legislative negotiations within the House Republican Party when, following the 2014 elections, a group of organized conservatives called the House Freedom Caucus regularly issued threats against its own party's leadership. Such behavior by an ideologically extreme bloc of lawmakers is not accounted for by existing theories of legislative politics. This Element posits explanations for why such threat-making might occur and what might increase its likelihood of success, then tests those explanations using the Freedom Caucus as a case study.

ISBNs: 978-1-108-73581-0 (PB), 9781108677011 (OC)
ISSNs: 2515-1606 (online), 2515-1592 (print)

# Contents

## 1 Threat-Making and Bargaining in Congress

In Congress, you get along by going along. This was the famous mantra of Sam Rayburn (D-TX), Speaker of the U.S. House of Representatives in the mid-twentieth century, who repeated it to freshly elected members of his chamber. It had a utilitarian purpose, encouraging freshmen to defer to older and more-senior lawmakers, but it also reflected the conventional wisdom that cooperation and compromise were more likely to result in legislative accomplishments than rebellion or stubbornness.[1]

A half-century after Rayburn's death, a new group emerged in Congress that appeared to follow the opposite tack. The House Freedom Caucus, which was founded by nine Republicans in January 2015 and quickly grew to about forty members, took strong conservative positions and insisted that GOP leaders modify legislation and floor rules closer to its liking. It became known for threatening to defeat bills and procedural motions of its own party, and for carrying out those threats – even at the risk of helping the minority party.

The Freedom Caucus's threat-making was criticized by some for being counterproductive and praised by others as a genuine effort to make the Republican Party stay true to its ideological principles. But beyond this normative debate over tactics, the hardball bargaining strategy of the Caucus raises two larger interrelated questions about legislative politics. First, why would a group of lawmakers from the far wing of a congressional party reject Rayburn's advice, not to mention the powerful political norms and incentives that encourage party loyalty, and employ threats to defect against its own party's leadership? Second, under what circumstances, if any, are such threats most likely to work?

The answer I offer to the first question is that, while the Freedom Caucus in many ways resembles other groups of like-minded lawmakers in Congress, certain electoral, partisan, and influence-related factors made the group uniquely predisposed to pursue aggressive bargaining tactics. Drawing upon new qualitative and quantitative data to answer the second question, I show that the effectiveness of the Freedom Caucus's hard-nosed tactics was determined by the group's size and unity, its organizational characteristics, its members' preferences, and its reputation for carrying out those threats. However, the Caucus's aggressive bargaining tactics were more effective at blocking bills or forcing votes than bringing about positive policy change, and its victories were not costless.

These findings not only shed light on the motivation and influence of the Freedom Caucus but also suggest at least a partial caveat to Rayburn's credo:

---

[1] Rayburn's quote is taken from Eigen and Siegel (1993).

sometimes, *not* going along may be a more fruitful course of action for law-makers. They are also a reminder that, even in a time of extreme partisanship and political polarization, American congressional parties are "big tent" institutions with considerable diversity among their membership, making them perennially vulnerable to dissent from internal factions. Keeping those factions satisfied is a continuous task that relies on careful coalition management by party leaders, who must deal with the preferences and predilections of faction members as well as broader political forces.

Before examining the Freedom Caucus in detail, I dedicate the rest of this section to a discussion of how modifications to existing models of bargaining and legislative voting behavior can explain why a group of lawmakers from the far wing of its party might be both willing and able to use threats to influence outcomes. I also offer hypotheses about the factors that should make those threats potent and credible, and thereby most likely to succeed.

## 1.1 The Logic of Legislative Threat-Making

Bargaining is a central feature of any legislature. A great deal of legislative bargaining follows a distributive or "share the wealth" model, wherein a set of benefits can be divided among the negotiating parties to build a majority coalition (Baron and Ferejohn 1989). However, not all legislative bargaining can be resolved so simply. Disputes can emerge, for example, over what constitutes a fair distribution of divisible benefits. Bills on issues like abortion may offer only nondivisible gains, creating a "winner-take-all" scenario in which the stakes for failure are high. Constituents may put pressure on their representatives or party leaders not to compromise on dearly held policy views. Lawmakers may be tempted to cast a position-taking vote against an agreement and thereby earn accolades from voters, even if it sacrifices their policy goals (Binder and Lee 2016).

Integrative approaches to bargaining – offering players side-payments or expanding the benefits available to the negotiating parties – can help overcome these roadblocks to agreement (Binder and Lee 2016). But if neither a distributive nor an integrative approach is available or acceptable, a congressional party or other group of lawmakers may instead resort to *threats*, promising to undertake an action if its demands are not met that would yield a negative outcome for all sides, in the hopes of intimidating opponents to accede to those demands (Schelling 1960). Threats, implicit or explicit, have long been a part of congressional life and may explain a range of policy and procedural outcomes, such as the restraint senators demonstrated through the early twentieth century by not using the filibuster (Schickler and Wawro 2006). But the conditions that discourage negotiated agreements in today's Congress also create incentives for congressional parties to employ threats. For instance, many voters balk at any effort at compromise by their favored political party and encourage it to maintain all-or-nothing demands. Even if threats fail to yield policy victory, they offer an opportunity for partisan position-taking to win votes in the next election (Mayhew 1974). As a result, Congress not only "labors under remarkably high barriers to success in negotiations" (Binder and Lee 2016, 113) but has been characterized by threat-making between Republicans and Democrats in recent years. Government shutdowns have been threatened, and sometimes carried out, by both parties in hopes of forcing their partisan opponents to accede to their policy demands. When the federal debt limit nearly reached its limit in 2011 and 2013, some Republicans seriously entertained the idea of allowing the limit to be breached unless Democrats agreed to major spending cuts.[2]

While threats between congressional parties are perhaps to be expected, they seem highly unlikely to happen within them. Just as they create barriers to successful policy negotiation across parties, greater party polarization and heightened partisan electoral competition should encourage internal unity. Lawmakers in a polarized legislature are far more likely to agree with the policy preferences of their own party's members than those of the other party, reducing the likelihood of cross-party voting (Rubin 2017). Partisan unity and effectiveness can help the party brand, improving the electoral future of its individual members. Informal norms also discourage rebellion, while party leaders have numerous tools at their disposal to enforce party discipline and deter defection, such as the selection of committee chairs and the distribution of campaign funding (Cox and McCubbins 1993, 2005; Froman and Ripley 1965; Pearson 2015; Smith 2007).

Yet even in today's polarized environment, disagreements within political parties are frequent. Congress's single-member districts create incentives to focus on the policy preferences of one's constituents, which may differ from those of the party as a whole. Committed constituents may demand that their representatives eschew compromise on matters of principle, even with their own party's leaders. Congressional leaders' formal powers are not without limits, and the use of punishments can easily backfire, while informal norms of partisan unity are less durable and harder to enforce than formal rules

---

[2] This behavior has sometimes been called *brinkmanship*. But in game theoretic terms, brinkmanship involves promises of future action that may lead to a negative outcome outside the control of the threatening party (what is known as a "probabilistic threat"), whereas threats are promises of future action that will result in a negative outcome with greater certainty (Schelling 1960).

(Green and Bee 2016). In addition, the same factors that discourage cross-party integrative solutions to conflict can also discourage such solutions within parties. For example, some policy or political objectives on which members of the same party disagree may be difficult to divide (think pro-life Democrats or pro-choice Republicans). Thus, threats to defect, not to mention actual defection,[3] can occur within as well as between congressional parties.

## 1.2 Intraparty Threats by Extremist Factions

Which members of a political party are most likely to disagree with, and thus threaten to dissent from, their leaders and colleagues? Since floor outcomes in the House are determined by majority vote, spatial models of voting predict that the median lawmaker will serve as the "pivotal player" who is most tempted to vote with the opposite party and decide vote outcomes (Black 1958; Cox and McCubbins 2005; Krehbiel 1998). This can be extended from a single legislator to a group, for if the group includes the median lawmaker, its members may have preferences that are "functionally indistinguishable" from the median member and thus act collectively as the pivotal player (Rubin 2017). Studies have confirmed that legislators closer to the floor median member are more likely to defect and less responsive to entreaties from majority-party leaders to vote with their party on legislation (Carson, Crespin, and Madonna 2014; Clarke, Jenkins, and Monroe 2016). There are also multiple examples in congressional history of groups that were influential because their members were close enough to the median legislator and sufficiently numerous to be "swing" votes, like the Republican insurgents of the 1910s and the Southern Delegations of the mid-twentieth century (Rubin 2017).

However, while spatial models predict that ideological moderates are the natural source of dissention (and threats to dissent) from their party, a bloc of lawmakers from the far wing of their party could also be theoretically tempted to threaten defection if policy-making is less salient to them than other, countervailing goals (Fenno 1973; Mayhew 1974). Legislators who care more about re-election, for example, may find that the electoral rewards of threatening to vote against their party (and doing so, if necessary) are greater than helping shift policy closer to their ideal preference point. Positive news stories from partisan news outlets, campaign donations from party activists, and pressure from primary voters to refrain from compromise may tempt more-extreme,

---

[3] I assume that lawmakers who could defect from their party will not necessarily do so, but instead find greater strategic advantages in threatening defection first. In section 2, I explain why this assumption holds for the Freedom Caucus.

re-election–minded members of Congress to threaten intraparty dissent. Ideologically distant lawmakers may care enough about another goal, internal influence, to vote against their perceived policy preferences (and especially against restrictive procedures) in order to expand their ability to shape legislation. As I explain in section 2, both electoral and influence-related incentives to dissent were present in the mid-2010s House of Representatives.[4]

Even if policy preferences are of greater consideration to party extremists than re-election or internal influence, a departure from one supposition underlying the spatial model allows for the possibility that a group of dissenters from the far wing of their party might still find it preferable to reject a leadership policy proposal and thus issue threats to defect. Specifically, if one relaxes the assumption that all legislators use the same standard, objective criteria to calculate the distance between the status quo and an alternative policy proposal, it follows that different lawmakers may evaluate the distance between the status quo point and a policy proposal differently, especially relative to their own ideal preference points. From the point of view of an extremist bloc within the majority party, a leadership proposal that is only marginally closer to their collective preferences than the status quo may be perceived as essentially no different from the status quo. (Ideologically moderate lawmakers could have the same perception problem, though it seems likely that they would have preferences close to the policy status quo and thus better discern the differences between a leadership proposal and the status quo.) This is particularly likely to occur under divided party government or if the party lacks a super-majority in the Senate, because majority-party leaders will be tempted to pass more-moderate bills to avoid presidential vetoes or Senate filibusters.[5] As I note in the following section, both conditions describe the political environment at the time the House Freedom Caucus was formed (see also Krehbiel 1998).[6]

## 1.3 When Threats Work

It is one thing for a group within a congressional party to threaten defection, but quite another for that threat to be effective. The effectiveness of a threat

---

[4] Moving from a one-dimensional to a two-dimensional spatial model also allows for the possibility of building majority coalitions by appealing to lawmakers further from, rather than closer to, one's ideal point (Hammond and Miller 1987).

[5] Relaxing this assumption seems plausible insofar as political scientists themselves have yet to reach consensus on how best to measure status quo and alternative policy locations (e.g., Richman 2011).

[6] Clarke (n.d.) uses conservative interest group position-taking as a proxy for the conservatism of desired policy outcomes, whereas I use the stated preferences of caucus members or leaders themselves to determine intent.

depends upon two necessary conditions. The first is "potency," or the ability of the group issuing a threat to be able to inflict harm (Schelling 2006). In the legislative setting, threat potency from a bloc of lawmakers seeking to influence floor outcomes derives from several, often interrelated, factors. The bloc's *size* and *unity* determine the number of votes it can reliably command. A faction that is large and unified enough can swing the vote outcome one way or another if its demands are not met, rolling the majority party (passing a measure over its opposition) or "disappointing" it (defeating a measure it desires) (Jenkins and Monroe 2015; Rubin 2017). (Since larger groups are likely to be less unified, threat-making blocs will likely strive to have just enough members to minimize the tradeoff between size and unity.) The *internal characteristics* of a faction are another key source for potency. If the threatening group has adopted "institutional arrangements" or uses peer pressure to overcome collective action problems, or if the group limits its membership to those who are "motivationally committed" through shared preferences to vote together, they are more likely to be pivotal (Baer 2017; Clarke n.d.; Dixit and Nalebuff 1991; Rubin 2017, 12; Shepsle 1991). Internal characteristics are intertwined with size and unity, since smaller and more-unified blocs are more likely to accept more-restrictive rules governing membership and behavior.

The other source of threat effectiveness is "credibility," a believable commitment to issue a threat – or, put another way, a threat issued by the side most willing to say no (Binder and Lee 2016; Schelling 2006).[7] Threat credibility for a bloc of legislators may derive from several factors. One is its members' *revealed preferences*: a group with collective preferences that would be better satisfied (or hindered less) than its opponents' preferences by carrying out the threat can issue that threat more credibly. As noted previously, this usually describes party moderates but could also describe party extremists who believe they would gain more (or lose less) by carrying out a threat. Another is *internal characteristics* that shield the group from retaliation by party leaders for carrying out a threat. Finally, *reputation* may be a source of threat credibility. If an individual or group develops a reputation for not backing down from threats, its future threats will be believed more readily; conversely, a threat that is abandoned weakens one's credibility. Reputation is especially important if the preferences of a legislative bloc are concealed or misunderstood by its opponents, and may be further cultivated through "strategic irrationality," or inducing a belief that

---

[7] For more on credible commitments in (and beyond) legislative politics, see North and Weingast (1989) and Wallner (2015).

the bloc neither knows nor cares about the likely self-inflicted harm from carrying out the threat.

## 1.4 Conclusion

Compromise and cooperation are cornerstones of legislative politics, but there are circumstances under which hard-nosed bargaining may be a more politically appealing strategy, not only by one political party against the other but also by a bloc of legislators against its own party leaders. Though threats are most likely to be employed by a group of party moderates, a broader understanding of legislator goals and congressional voting behavior allows for the possibility that a group of party extremists could also use threat-making. However, threats are unlikely to succeed unless they are potent and credible.

In the next section, I introduce the House Freedom Caucus, an intraparty organization of ideological extremists that has regularly employed threats against its own party's leadership as a major part of negotiation strategy. The Caucus thus provides an opportunity to reveal the reasons for, and the possibilities and limitations of, using aggressive legislative bargaining.[8] I show that, based on its members' goals and the political context in which it formed, the group had incentives to use hard bargaining methods; and furthermore, its threats had the capacity to be both potent and credible enough to influence legislative outcomes.

## 2 A Brief Introduction to the House Freedom Caucus

In the previous section, I outlined the theoretical reasons that a group of lawmakers from the extreme wing of their party would be motivated to defect or threaten to defect, and I proposed several likely sources of threat potency and threat credibility. I now introduce an organized bloc of ideologically conservative Republicans from the 114th Congress, the House Freedom Caucus, as a case study to test these claims. First, I briefly review the events that led to the formation of the Freedom Caucus, how the group was organized, and key characteristics of its members. I then show that the theoretical explanations for an intraparty group from the far wing of the party to defect apply to the Caucus in the 114th Congress. I also provide evidence that the Caucus's size, organization, and other features made it uniquely positioned to issue effective threats against party leaders.

---

[8] The Caucus could thus possibly be considered a "deviant" case study, or a case that illustrates an unusual phenomenon of interest and thus valuable for identifying new causal explanations (Gerring 2006).

## 2.1 Intraparty Congressional Organizations and the House Freedom Caucus

The history of Congress is replete with examples of lawmakers forming into subgroups within or across party lines. One common type of subgroup is the *caucus*, an organized, policy-oriented, and relatively durable association not sanctioned by chamber or party rules. Caucuses may be organized along partisan dimensions, with same-party members who share common ideological views and policy goals, which Ruth Bloch Rubin terms *intraparty organizations* (Hammond 1998; Rubin 2017). Notable intraparty congressional organizations of the past include the House progressive caucus of the early 1900s, the Southern Caucus of the Senate from the 1930s through 1960s, the Democratic Study Group (DSG), formed in 1959, and the Conservative Opportunity Society, created in 1983 (Baer 2017; Hammond 1998; Kofmehl 1964; Rubin 2017). Most intraparty organizations have either had members from the moderate wing of their party, making them likely pivotal voters on the chamber floor, or have been large enough to dictate internal party policy. Some, however, have been smaller groups consisting of more ideologically extreme lawmakers – including the House Freedom Caucus.

Starting in 2011, the House Republican Conference was plagued by intraparty conflicts between, on the one hand, its more-conservative and junior members – many of whom were affiliated with the Tea Party movement and pressed for confrontation with President Barack Obama to achieve their policy objectives – and, on the other hand, its more-senior and moderate members who did not (Draper 2012; Green 2016; Green and Bee 2016). A Tea Party Caucus of conservative Republicans was swiftly established, boasting about five dozen members at its height (Travis 2011). Though that group would fall into decline, intraparty discontent remained, fed by President Obama's re-election in 2012, Speaker John Boehner's (R-OH) predilection for striking deals with minority-party Democrats, limited influence by the rank-and-file in procedural and policy-making decisions, and the election of brash new conservatives to the House in 2012 and 2014.[9]

The formation of the House Freedom Caucus followed a pattern similar to prior intraparty organizations, emerging when a faction of lawmakers possessing unmet legislative goals felt dissatisfaction with their party and its leaders (Hammond 1998; Rubin 2017). The seeds of the group were sown by

---

[9] For more on the intraparty conflict between Boehner and GOP conservatives that preceded the formation of the Freedom Caucus, see Alberta (2017b) and Draper (2012). Boehner's initial reticence in punishing intraparty dissent may have eroded the "reputation for toughness" a party needs to temper rebellion (Cox and McCubbins 1994, 222; see also section 5).

the November 2014 election for chair of the Republican Study Committee (RSC), the party's long-standing conservative intraparty organization, which right-leaning candidate Mick Mulvaney (R-SC) lost amid allegations of interference by the GOP leadership (Lizza 2015; Newhauser 2014). Shortly thereafter, the House voted on a "cromnibus" funding bill that had been negotiated by Republican leaders and was disliked by most conservatives. Frustrated by these events, Mulvaney and eight other congressional members formed a new, independent group of their own in January 2015, which they named the Freedom Caucus (Will 2017).[10]

In addition to the reasons behind its creation, and that all its members were from one political party, the Freedom Caucus had other similarities to previous intraparty congressional organizations. Like other partisan caucuses, the group was oriented towards shared policy objectives, as was made explicit by its mission statement, which endorsed "limited government" and "policies that promote the liberty, safety, and prosperity of all Americans" (Jordan 2015). Its founding members were more conservative than the party average,[11] and in interviews and press releases they touted the group's focus on enacting right-leaning policy. For instance, Caucus co-founder Raúl Labrador (R-ID) stated that their intent was to negotiate with leadership to "push the entire conference to the right," which meant "we go ahead and sit down with leadership and let them know what we want, why we want it, [and] what ideas we have to improve the product or the process" (Gehrke 2015a).[12] As with other intraparty congressional organizations, the Caucus was also well-organized, with a clear structure and set of bylaws. It was led by a board of directors consisting of the group's founders, which in turn nominated a chairman subject to election by the full group for a one-year term.[13] The Caucus levied dues on its members, allowing it to hire a small staff (Bade 2016c; McPherson 2016). It also held regular members-only meetings, and within six months the Caucus had

---

[10] The caucus held its first meeting on January 12, 2015 and announced its formation on January 26 (Disler 2015). Its nine founding members included Justin Amash (R-MI), Ron DeSantis (R-FL), John Fleming (R-LA), Scott Garrett (R-NJ), Jim Jordan (R-OH), Raúl Labrador (R-ID), Mark Meadows (R-NC), Mick Mulvaney (R-SC), and Matt Salmon (R-AZ) (Gehrke 2015a).

[11] The average first-dimension DW-NOMINATE scores from the 113th Congress of the nine Caucus founders was 0.676, versus the GOP average of 0.484. All but one of the founders had first-dimension DW-NOMINATE scores at or above the 80th percentile for the party. See also Clarke (n.d., 9–10).

[12] See also Meadows 2015. Some have called the Freedom Caucus the spirit of the Tea Party or the Tea Party "wing" of the GOP (e.g., "House Freedom Caucus Helps Define Tense Power Dynamic in Congress"; Laslo 2016). But this is somewhat misleading. The Tea Party movement had lost much of its luster by 2015, and only seven Tea Party Caucus members from 2011, when the group was at its largest, joined the House Freedom Caucus four years later.

[13] The Caucus's first chair, Jim Jordan (R-OH), was re-elected to serve a second one-year term in November 2015 (DeBonis 2015c).

established a means of counting members' vote preferences on upcoming measures, as well as determining the sentiment of "members in the orbit" of the Caucus.[14] It would even develop a smart phone app allowing Caucus leaders to immediately gauge other members' positions (French 2015c; Fuller 2017a; Rubin 2017).

There were some significant differences between the House Freedom Caucus and a typical intraparty organization, however. For one thing, its bylaws included a formal binding mechanism: the Caucus's full membership could be bound to an official position if 80 percent of its members voted in favor of that position. In addition, while many intraparty organizations have sought to maximize their size, such as by offering credit-claiming incentives to would-be members (Rubin 2017), the Freedom Caucus was an invite-only group that deliberately capped its size to about forty Republicans (Clarke n. d.; French 2015c), and it kept its membership roll private.[15] [In terms of demographics, HFC members were also more likely to represent districts in the South (56%, versus 45% of non-HFC Republican districts) and West (22%, compared with 10% of non-HFC members), though the average age and income, and ethnic makeup, of their constituents was nearly identical (DeSilver 2015a, 2015b).] The group also focused on shaping existing procedure and policy, as opposed to developing alternative policy proposals, as was the objective of such noteworthy intraparty organizations as the DSG and the RSC.[16] Most importantly, the Freedom Caucus was unusual in its embrace of threat-making and other aggressive bargaining tactics against Republican leaders. Within a year after it was formed, the group was known by many as the "Caucus of [Hell] No" and was believed to have brought down Speaker Boehner by threatening a floor motion to declare the speakership vacant. Threats by individual or loosely organized lawmakers certainly happen, but rarely have organized groups of party extremists in Congress used threats or aggressive negotiations against their own party's leaders, and certainly not to the same degree or frequency as the Freedom Caucus.[17] The DSG, for instance, sought at least tacit approval from party leaders or a majority of the Democratic

---

[14] Interview with congressional aide, February 22, 2018.

[15] Nonetheless, as noted below, it did not take long for the Caucus's membership to become public. Some Freedom Caucus members may have had an incentive to reveal their membership to cultivate an image that "they are willing to fight harder" and repudiate their own party's leaders (Herszenhorn 2015).

[16] For more on the Caucus's rules and organization, see Clarke (n.d.) and Rubin (2017).

[17] Intraparty organizations in the past have either been composed of party moderates (e.g., the Southern Delegations) or ensured they had at least the tacit support of party leaders before employing aggressive tactics [e.g., the Democratic Study Group (Rubin 2017)]. There are examples of lawmakers who have used such threats but not as members of organized groups (e.g., junior House Republicans in the 105th Congress).

Caucus before pushing for civil rights legislation or procedural changes that would empower House liberals (Rubin 2017). With no intraparty group truly comparable to the Freedom Caucus in modern congressional history,[18] the Caucus is especially valuable as a case study of the causes and consequences of hard-nosed bargaining in Congress.

## 2.2 Motivation for Defection

Recall from section 1 that two conditions may create an incentive for the far ideological wing of a congressional party to threaten defection. One is when party leaders offer policy proposals that are perceived as indistinguishable from the status quo because, from the point of view of the party's most ideologically extreme members, they are too moderate. This was a probable outcome during the Freedom Caucus's first two years of existence. Because Democrats controlled the White House and could filibuster bills in the Senate, House Republican leaders had a strong motivation to pass bills that were more moderate and thus likely to pass the Senate and be signed into law (see also Krehbiel 1998). However, doing so meant that legislation would come up for a vote on the House floor that was so distant from the legislative preferences of party conservatives as to be effectively identical, from their perspective, to the policy status quo. One early example from 2015 was a border security bill that tightened immigration controls, but which Caucus members disliked in part because it did not attempt to deport undocumented workers or address Obama's executive order easing the enforcement of certain immigration rules (see section 3).

The sincere policy preferences of lawmakers are difficult to determine, and one cannot definitively reject the possibility that the Caucus's declared preferences were not genuine but rather a tactical move designed to win re-election or extract concessions from party leaders. But there is evidence that at least implies that the group's members held genuinely conservative preferences and were willing to act on behalf of those preferences, including voting against GOP policy proposals. One study found that Freedom Caucus members were more likely to vote against the majority of the majority party in the 114th Congress when legislative proposals were more moderate (Clarke n.d.). Preparing to leave Congress after having lost his gubernatorial primary, Raúl Labrador admitted that GOP voters are "not ideologically pure like some of us" (Alberta 2018). In anonymous interviews with the author, Caucus members

---

[18] One possible historical example is when Democratic Party's "liberal bloc" of the 1930s tried to force the House Rules Committee to release a wage bill by threatening to join minority party Republicans in a cross-party coalition to block Democratic bills ("Labor Bloc Maps Wage Bill Revolt"; Paulsen 1959). Another occurred in 1970, when the RSC attempted to circumvent GOP leaders and kill a Nixon welfare reform bill (Rubin 2017).

insisted their policy views were genuinely held and they were disinclined to compromise them. "We actually believe we have some serious issues that face us," said one Freedom Caucus Republican when asked why others were not willing to oppose leadership bills. The group, said another member, was conceived as "a tactical way to enact our principles," and could reach consensus in internal deliberations because "no one's questioning anyone's conservative credentials."[19]

The other condition under which a more ideologically extreme set of lawmakers possesses an incentive to threaten intraparty defection is if it has countervailing nonpolicy goals. One objective after the 2014 elections that incentivized defection for conservative Republicans was re-election. A record number of primary challengers to House Republicans had based their campaigns on claims that the incumbent was insufficiently right-leaning, putting pressure on those incumbents to prove their ideological *bona fides* (Boatright 2014). Freedom Caucus districts were, on average, slightly more Republican than the median GOP district, giving Caucus members an additional incentive to position themselves further to the right (Bialik and Bycoffe 2015). In addition, the GOP was more ideologically focused than the Democratic Party (Grossman and Hopkins 2016). Conservative voters at the time were also more rigidly opposed to compromise: one survey from mid-2014 revealed that they were far more likely than liberals to insist their elected representatives "stick to their positions," perhaps because, according to one study, they were loss-averse to a greater degree than liberals (Glaser and Berry 2018; Pew Research Center 2014). Furthermore, GOP leaders, particularly Speaker Boehner, were not popular with Republican voters (see section 4). Meanwhile, right-leaning media web sites provided positive coverage of "true" conservatives in Congress, and ideological interest groups such as FreedomWorks and Heritage Action gave praise and campaign donations to those deemed sufficiently rightward-leaning (Draper 2012; Mann and Ornstein 2012; Strong 2013). One congressional aide familiar with the workings of the Caucus explained that "these are members who are very responsive to their constituents," many of whom were frustrated that "D.C. had failed them ... over and over again." According to one Caucus member, "the members of the Freedom Caucus take the word 'representative' probably a little more literally than the average member of Congress."[20] Indeed, a common theme of public statements by Caucus leaders was the need to keep campaign promises made to voters.[21]

---

[19] Interviews with Freedom Caucus members, February 16 and March 6, 2018.

[20] Interviews with congressional aide, February 22, 2018, and with Freedom Caucus member, March 6, 2018.

[21] See, for example, Corombos 2015, Jordan and Meadows 2017, and King 2017.

Internal influence was another objective of Freedom Caucus members that incentivized dissent. As previously noted, the group got its start after Mick Mulvaney lost the election for RSC chair over a leadership-backed candidate; but more fundamentally, the Caucus's founders and many of its members were motivated by deep mistrust in their leaders and frustration at being excluded from party decision making. In the 114th Congress, few members of the Caucus occupied positions of influence in the Republican Conference: there were none on the powerful Ways and Means Committee, and just one served on Appropriations. The group's committee influence was largely concentrated on the less-influential Oversight Committee, nearly half (48%) of whose Republican members and four of its subcommittee chairs were from the Freedom Caucus. Furthermore, though the bloc started the 114th Congress with one member on the GOP's steering committee [Cynthia Lummis (R-WY)] and five who were whips,[22] no Caucus Republicans served in the top ranks of leadership (Hawkings 2015). Explained Raúl Labrador, "That's the whole purpose of the organization. We have a lot of people here who feel they are not being heard" (Fuller 2015a). The focus on internal influence made the group particularly sensitive to the ways that congressional procedure excluded them from opportunities to shape bills. "Our guys have always been more about the process than the policy," said one Caucus member.[23]

It should also be noted that Freedom Caucus members had other characteristics that made them preternaturally inclined to use aggressive bargaining tactics. The average member was more junior than the median House Republican – over 70% had served three terms or fewer, versus just over half of non-Caucus Republicans – and thus less likely to be inculcated into the norms of party loyalty and vote with party leaders, though HFC members were only slightly younger (54) than their non-HFC counterparts (56) (Bialik and Bycoffe 2015; DeSilver 2015a; Green 2016). Jim Jordan (D-OH), the first chair of the Caucus, subscribed to a confrontational approach to politics, at least against partisan opponents, stating that he wanted Republicans to go toe-to-toe with Democrats to make them "blink" rather than negotiate with them to pass more-moderate legislation (Bade 2016d). Similarly, Mark Meadows (R-SC), who later became the group's second chairman, initiated an effort in 2013 to make party leaders eliminate Obamacare funding in all future spending bills, forcing Obama and Senate Democrats to comply by shutting down the government if necessary

---

[22] The five were Ron DeSantis (FL), Jeff Duncan (SC), Trent Franks (AZ), Cynthia Lummis (WY), and Steve Pearce (NM).

[23] Interview with Freedom Caucus member, February 16, 2018.

("U.S. Rep. Mark Meadows Sends Letter"). Caucus members' willingness to defy their own party leaders was especially pronounced. Mulvaney had run for RSC chair on a platform of keeping the group from becoming what he bluntly described as a "shill for leadership" (Fuller 2014), and the prior voting records of the Caucus's founders and members suggested a remarkable fearlessness about openly challenging the authority of the Speaker and other GOP leaders.[24] This would be particularly important in explaining why Caucus members were more willing than their partisan brethren to vote against not only their party's policy-making authority (i.e., bills and amendments) but also its procedural and organizational authority by rejecting floor rules and, in one instance, the right of John Boehner to remain Speaker of the House (Cox and McCubbins 1993, 2005; Jenkins and Stewart 2013; see also section 4).[25]

I have framed the Freedom Caucus as an intraparty organization inclined to threaten defection, but what if its members' ideological conservatism and nonpolicy goals meant they would vote against GOP bills and rules regardless of what party leaders offered in any negotiations? Some scholars have considered the bloc from this perspective (e.g., Clarke n.d.), and many of its critics claimed that it was inherently oppositional. For instance, Ted Poe (R-TX), who left the Caucus in 2017, complained that "some members" would "vote no against the Ten Commandments if it came up for a vote" (Savransky 2017). However, the group's policy-oriented mission statement and the remarks of other Freedom Caucus members suggest the group genuinely hoped that threats to vote against bills and procedural rules, whether implicit or explicit, would convince Republican leaders to give the Caucus more influence and legislate more conservatively and aggressively. As Caucus member Matt Salmon (R-AZ) insisted, "We're not the caucus of no. We're a group trying to get to yes" (French and Kim 2015). Another member of the group told the author that members "have to be able to say no to leadership, and . . . also have to be willing

---

[24] Over a dozen future Caucus members did vote (or were considered likely to vote) against Boehner for Speaker in 2013 (Reeve 2013); two years later, three of the founding members voted against Boehner for Speaker (Amash, Garrett, Meadows) along with a dozen other lawmakers who later joined the Caucus. The founders' second-dimension DW-NOMINATE scores, which may capture antiestablishmentarian tendencies (Voteview 2015), were also near the party extreme: eight of the nine had scores in the 113th Congress that were at or above the 70th percentile for the GOP. For more on how lawmakers may adopt assertive nonvoting tactics to achieve their objectives, see Theriault 2013.

[25] Threat-making may have also been encouraged in the 114th Congress by the Caucus's seeming lack of concern about "penalty defaults" for legislative inaction (like government shutdowns) and the absence of a same-party president who could help enforce party unity (Binder and Lee 2016).

to say yes."[26] In addition, as will be seen in the next section, while the Caucus was sometimes oblique about its intentions, it usually made its opposition to legislation and procedural rules sufficiently clear and far enough in advance that GOP leaders had the opportunity to respond to its demands, and sometimes demonstrated a good-faith effort to vote with the rest of the party if those demands were at least partially met. It may be more accurate to say the group was less a "caucus of no" than a caucus that would not take no for an answer.

## 2.3 Why Freedom Caucus Threats Could Be Effective

If the House Freedom Caucus had multiple incentives to employ threats against GOP leaders as part of its bargaining strategy, what would make those threats effective? In section 1, I identified several factors that can yield greater leverage for a threat-making faction, including sufficient size and unity to determine floor votes, internal mechanisms to foster unity and provide protection from retaliation, a membership whose preferences could plausibly be satisfied (or less unsatisfied) by carrying out a threat, and a reputation for carrying out threats. Though those factors were not always present in individual instances of threat-making (see section 3), in a general sense they all applied to the Freedom Caucus in the 114th Congress, and they often reinforced each other.

Consider first the potential potency of the Freedom Caucus's threats. At the time of its formation, the party balance in Congress was 246 Republicans and 188 Democrats (plus one vacancy). By early February 2015, the Caucus had gained the minimum thirty members necessary to vote with a unified Democratic minority to deny the GOP a floor majority, and its membership peaked at nearly forty by early spring (Disler 2015; French 2015c; Fuller 2015a).[27] According to one Caucus member, the group could also, depending on the issue at hand, count on the votes of a dozen or more "affiliate"

---

[26] Interview with Freedom Caucus member, March 6, 2018.

[27] According to one account, 37 people attended the Freedom Caucus's first meeting (Disler 2015). Membership in the Caucus is derived from three sources that jointly identified 34 lawmakers as members in 2015 (DeSilver 2015a; Fuller 2015f, 2015i). Two of those lawmakers, Tom McClintock (CA) and Reid Ribble (NJ), resigned from the Caucus in 2015 and are counted as members until their departure dates. Texans Brian Babin and Ted Poe were not identified by DeSilver as Caucus members, but their membership was confirmed when they resigned from the group in early 2017. Two more identified by some but not all three sources [Randy Weber (TX) and Ted Yoho (FL)] are counted starting at the date of their earliest confirmed membership (September 15, 2015 for Yoho and October 15, 2015 for Weber). Another two Republicans joined the group in 2016: Joe Barton (TX), who did so relatively late and is excluded from the analysis, and Warren Davidson (OH), who joined shortly after winning a special election in June 2016.

lawmakers who were "aligned philosophically [with the Caucus] or will vote with us."[28] In addition, members of the Freedom Caucus who had served in the previous (113th) Congress had demonstrated remarkable solidarity, voting unanimously on 61.3 percent of all roll call votes with an average Rice cohesion score of 0.869 (slightly below the average 0.873 Rice score of non-Caucus Republicans).[29] Freedom Caucus members also recognized that their unity, particularly in opposition to unwanted measures, was key to their influence. Scott Perry (PA), for instance, observed that "when you're a minority in an organization, your strength is in sticking together," and Mark Meadows argued that the power of the Caucus is "the power of negation" (Bade, Dawsey, and Haberkorn 2017; Douglas 2017).

Interestingly, the group would prove somewhat less unified in the 114th Congress. Though its members voted together unanimously on virtually the same percentage of all roll call votes (61.1%) as its future members did in the previous Congress, its members' average Rice score fell from 0.869 to 0.746 (versus non-Caucus Republicans' score, which rose from 0.873 to 0.883).[30] Nonetheless, because the Freedom Caucus's membership was larger than the margin between the two parties in the 114th Congress, it could afford some defections and still be a pivotal bloc. Congress's high level of party polarization also meant that Republican leaders would struggle to win enough Democratic votes to compensate for Caucus opposition. In fact, minority Democrats would prove more unified in the 114th Congress than in the 113th Congress, with its average Rice score rising from 0.843 to 0.901. The Freedom Caucus was thus *potentially* pivotal – reversing floor outcomes had all its members switched their votes – for 62.3 percent (687) of all majoritarian floor votes in the 114th Congress (687), far more than the 50.0 percent (546) of majoritarian floor votes in which its future members were pivotal in the 113th.[31] The Caucus's size and unity, coupled with the unity of Democrats, thus meant it could plausibly form what could be termed "incidental majority coalitions," creating a floor majority against its own party by voting in the same direction as Democrats without

---

[28] Interview with Freedom Caucus member, March 6, 2018.

[29] The Rice cohesion score is the absolute difference between yes and no votes divided by the total number of votes cast. Thirty-four Freedom Caucus members from the 114th Congress served in the 113th Congress.

[30] The presence of freshmen appears to have reduced the group's degree of unity. When excluding the members of the Caucus in the 114th Congress who were not in the 113th Congress, the group voted together unanimously in 62.3 percent of all recorded votes in the 114th Congress, but its Rice cohesion score rose to 0.886.

[31] The difference is statistically significant (p < .001, two-tailed test). Considering just roll calls from June 20, 2015 (when the Freedom Caucus's maximum size was first confirmed publicly) to the end of the 114th Congress, the organization was pivotal on 66 percent of all roll call votes.

having to coordinate with the minority party in advance, and doing so to meet very different policy objectives.

Threat potency was further enhanced by certain organizational features of the Caucus that encouraged collective action.[32] The group could take a single bargaining position via official position statements and by delegating its chair or board members to be emissaries to the GOP leadership. Its regular meetings served as a forum to develop consensus on policy questions, hear from party leaders behind closed doors, and employ peer pressure to encourage potentially wayward members to stick together, all doubtless made easier by the group's small size (Clarke n.d.). One Freedom Caucus member explained that the group's influence rested in part on "be[ing] able to have the free flow of ideas and debate."[33] This was particularly important because, conventional wisdom notwithstanding, there could be considerable diversity of views within the bloc. The congressional aide quoted previously described the group as initially consisting of several distinct groups, including libertarians, Republicans who prioritized social conservatism, and "three-legged stool conservatives" who emphasized social and fiscal conservatism as well as a strong national defense.[34] "We have 40 conservatives with 40 different ideas," Raúl Labrador said, "and we're less successful because we're taking 40 different ideas to the leadership. It's better to have 40 conservatives working together to take one idea to the leadership" ("House Border Bill Pleases Neither Party"). As two journalists put it, the Freedom Caucus served as "a single voice to speak with publicly, and to negotiate with in private" (French and Kim 2015).

The Freedom Caucus took several additional steps to enhance its unity and protect its members from retaliation. Membership was by invitation only, which allowed the group to exclude any potential dissenters, maintain a manageable size, increase the probability that its members would share ideological preferences and strategic outlook, and reduce the necessity of forcing compliance with Caucus positions (Rubin 2017). As Mick Mulvaney explained, "what we told the guys we recruited into the Freedom Caucus was that you have to be able to" vote against procedural rules (Lizza 2015). In

---

[32] This was confirmed by one Caucus member, who told the author that the group's "bylaws, Constitution, and rules ... provide a framework for a cohesive Caucus" (Interview with Freedom Caucus member, March 6, 2018). Though beyond the scope of this study, Ruth Bloch Rubin's analysis of intraparty organizations suggests some of the conditions under which unity-building rules will be adopted, including sizeable membership, strong faction leaders, and members holding intense preferences on high-stakes salient issues like race relations or the power of the Speaker (Rubin 2017).

[33] Interview with Freedom Caucus member, March 6, 2018.

[34] Interview with congressional aide, February 22, 2018.

addition, the bloc imposed no formal sanctions on lawmakers wishing to exit from the group, so that would-be rebels would be more likely to leave the organization altogether rather than face formal or informal pressure to conform, and its bylaws permitted the ejection of members who voted consistently against the Caucus (Clarke 2017; Fuller 2015i; Rubin 2017). As a result, in the words of one Freedom Caucus member, "all the [people] in our group get along personally."[35] Its binding rule, which one Caucus member called "a critical component of our rules" (and which was only feasible because of the group's small size and relative ideological homogeneity), could also ensure that contrary members would fall in line and help it vote as a unit.[36]

One should not overstate the capacity of the Freedom Caucus to bind or otherwise influence its members to take positions contrary to their preferences. The 80 percent threshold for invoking the binding rule was high, precluding its frequent use and making it likely that, when it was employed, consensus was already within reach. "We designed the 80 percent rule to be difficult to achieve," explained Mulvaney. "It's very difficult for 80 percent of us to do anything" (Sherman and French 2015).[37] The group also granted each member two "free passes" to violate the binding rule.[38] And while the Caucus may have influenced some of its members in individual cases, it did not appear to sway legislators' vote choice in the aggregate. For instance, while they voted together unanimously for a sizeable 61.1 percent of all roll call votes in the 114th Congress, future Caucus members in the 113th Congress did so at a statistically indistinguishable rate of 61.3 percent, suggesting that Caucus membership was conformational, not determinative, of voting behavior. In addition, in the 113th Congress, future members voted against their party 57 times (4.8% of roll call votes), and though that number increased after the Caucus was formed in 2015 to 77 times (5.8% of all votes) the difference is not statistically significant ($p = .23$, two-tailed test).[39]

Another indication that the Caucus's power over lawmaker behavior may have been limited is that Republicans' vote choice was no more or less likely to be influenced by Caucus membership. For every recorded vote in the 114th Congress, I ran a logit regression analysis, with vote choice as the dependent

---

[35]  Interview with Freedom Caucus member, February 16, 2018.

[36]  The same member of the Caucus explained that the binding rule helped bring along dissenters by signaling "that the vast majority of the caucus supports" a certain position. Interview with Freedom Caucus member, March 6, 2018.

[37]  Similarly, the binding House Democratic Caucus of the 1910s often committed its members to vote together on matters for which they already largely agreed (Green 2002).

[38]  Interview with Freedom Caucus member, March 6, 2018.

[39]  This increase might also have been due to a leftward shift of the legislative agenda (Clarke n.d.).

variable, and included Caucus membership as an explanatory variable while controlling for other commonly cited predictors of voting behavior.[40] The same was done for the 113th, with a variable measuring whether a lawmaker was going to join the Caucus. The percentage of votes in the 114th Congress for which Caucus membership was statistically significant was 14.4 percent (190 votes), higher than what one would expect if the frequency was due to chance,[41] but was actually *lower* than the percentage of votes in the 113th Congress for which future Caucus membership was statistically significant (18.8%, or 225 votes), a statistically significant difference (p = .003, two-tailed test).

Besides potency, the other ingredient of an effective threat is credibility – the likelihood that a threat will be carried out – and here too the organization had several advantages. As previously noted, Freedom Caucus Republicans both were conservative and had rebellious tendencies, lending greater plausibility to the group's threats to defect. The Caucus also quickly acquired a reputation for carrying out its threats. As early as January 2015, the group was implicated in a large conservative revolt against a border security bill, which forced GOP leaders to pull the bill, and by mid-2015, when it nearly sank a procedural rule for consideration trade legislation, it was widely known for following through on threats to oppose measures desired by the Republican leadership (see section 3). As Caucus member Matt Salmon (AZ) warned in mid-July 2015, GOP leaders "have to realize what motivates us and that *there are consequences if you cross a line*" (French 2015c, emphasis added). The Caucus may have even employed strategic irrationality to bolster its credibility. Mick Mulvaney recalled an early conversation over the debt limit with Majority Leader Kevin McCarthy (R-CA) in which McCarthy told Mulvaney that "we don't want to play chicken on this issue." Mulvaney responded, "Put this issue aside, I'll play chicken with you every time. *You think I am crazy, and I know you are not*" (Herszenhorn 2015, emphasis added).

Internal rules and other mechanisms were also adopted by the Freedom Caucus to help protect members from retaliation and thus make them more likely to carry out a threat to defect, though their effectiveness was not always clear. The group kept its membership secret and was the only ideological

---

[40] Controls included ideology (estimated with first- and second-dimension NOMINATE scores), terms served in office, service in party leadership, service as a committee chair, and southern representation. Hammond (1998) conducts a similar analysis to test the influence of congressional caucuses more generally.

[41] This was confirmed by rerunning the regression analysis 100 times with randomly selected groups of Republicans of the same size as the Freedom Caucus; membership in those groups was statistically significant in an average 5.3 percent of roll call votes.

member group in the 114th Congress lacking a public website (Eno 2017; "House Freedom Caucus Helps Define Tense Power Dynamic in Congress"). However, enterprising reporters soon managed to determine and publicize the group's membership. It also developed its own fundraising networks and formed at least one political action committee to provide financial support to those denied funds by vengeful party leaders (McGee 2017).[42] "You have to create a support system for members" so they "can survive without" the help of leaders, as the aide quoted previously put it.[43] But it would be challenging for the group to compensate for the loss of the many electoral resources provided by party leadership – not just direct contributions, but money from leader-allied political action committees as well – a problem I return to in section 5.

## 2.4 Conclusion

The Freedom Caucus had strong incentives to pursue hard bargaining in the 114th Congress, a result of divided party control of the national government, external pressures on conservative Republicans to maintain uncompromising positions, the unpopularity of GOP leaders, Caucus members' lack of traditional avenues of influence, and the ideological leanings and confrontational style of its members. The group's threats could be both potent, thanks to its size, high level of internal cohesion, and unity-inducing mechanisms; and credible, thanks to its members' policy preferences, the bloc's reputation for rebellion, and its efforts to protect members from retaliation. Whether these threats worked is another matter. In the next section, I analyze newly collected data on the activities of the Freedom Caucus to answer that question.

## 3 The Influence of the House Freedom Caucus

I now use the behavior of the House Freedom Caucus in the 114th Congress (2015–16) as a means of determining the efficacy of aggressive bargaining tactics in the U.S. Congress. Specifically, I review individual instances in which the Caucus sought to achieve its expressed objectives on legislation and procedural rules, evaluating the extent to which the group's successes were the consequence of persuasive threats issued under favorable conditions.

## 3.1 Finding and Testing Cases of Freedom Caucus Influence

At first glance, it would seem that the Freedom Caucus was not especially influential at shaping vote outcomes on the House floor. Only twice in the 114th

---

[42] The political action committee gave the Freedom Caucus a means of recruiting new congressional candidates as well; see section 5.

[43] Interview with congressional aide, February 22, 2018.

Congress did the group "disappoint" its own party by defeating a proposal supported by a majority of the Republican Conference (Clarke, Jenkins, and Monroe 2017). This low success rate is misleading, however. The Caucus exercised its influence selectively; for instance, one study found that the group was more likely to be disloyal on certain procedural motions, not all votes (Den Hartog and Nokken 2017). The group also may have been able to alter bills or rules before they came to the floor or to keep some measures from being brought up for a vote altogether. In addition, the political significance of its victories outweighed their infrequency. One of the two "disappointment" votes led to the defeat of a funding bill for the Department of Homeland Security in February 2015, which forced GOP leaders to renegotiate funding for the agency, signaled that the Caucus was willing to defy party leadership, and instigated rumors that Boehner's speakership was under threat (see below).[44]

Instead of relying on recorded floor votes to test Caucus influence, I created an original data set of cases in which the group tried to shape legislative outcomes. I drew from two sources to identify these cases. The first is the 13 public positions taken by the Caucus in the 114th Congress on House-related legislative and procedural proposals. The second is a "sweep" of major news media outlets (Mayhew 2005), identified via Google news alerts and the Lexis-Nexis newspaper database, for claims from at least two distinct news reports that the bloc exercised or attempted to exercise political influence.[45] These claims include the Caucus's members or chairman taking a position on a bill or proposal, negotiating with party leaders over the content of legislation or the procedures governing consideration of a bill, or convening the Caucus to consider taking a position on a particular rule or legislative measure. For both the public position-taking data and news reports, I used bill tracking and media accounts to determine the ultimate outcome of Caucus activity.

These two sets of data are not without limitations. Press stories and public Caucus statements cannot capture efforts at influence by the group that were hidden from view, nor measures kept off the floor by party leaders who anticipated Caucus opposition before it emerged. Threats can be oblique, making it hard to know when threat-making is taking place, and a lack of

---

[44] The other "disappointment" vote was the rejection of an amendment to H.R. 4909 on May 18, 2016.

[45] Google news alerts were captured daily between January 1, 2015 and December 31, 2016. To ensure the veracity of these reports and that no allegations of Freedom Caucus influence were omitted, I also conducted a Lexis-Nexis search of news stories from the *Washington Post, New York Times, Politico, Roll Call*, and *The Hill* published over the same time span, using the search term "House Freedom Caucus."

data on internal Caucus deliberations and negotiations between party and Caucus leaders limits the ability to analyze specific bargaining tactics. In addition, perhaps only when the bloc felt that success was more likely – because the issue was high-profile, for instance, or because the views of Republican voters differed dramatically from those of party leaders – did it pursue hard-nosed bargaining. However, I find sufficient variation in success rates for the Freedom Caucus to suggest that it was willing to fight on behalf of issues for which victory was not assured. More generally, the use of publicly known instances of attempted influence have the advantage of determining the group's success rate when it actually tried to exercise influence (versus, say, roll call votes on which the Caucus did not take a position), and it also allows one to identify reasons for its success or failure.[46] In addition, while the number of instances of attempted influence uncovered by this method (18) constitutes a small percentage of the number of bills considered in the 114th Congress, they involved many high-profile and substantive matters. Of the 27 legislative measures identified by the journal *Congressional Quarterly* (*CQ*) as the most significant of the 114th Congress, the Freedom Caucus was involved with one-third of them, and just under a quarter (six) of 26 *CQ*-identified "key" recorded floor votes.[47]

Table 1 lists the 11 (of 18) instances for which the Freedom Caucus can plausibly be credited with bringing about an outcome favorable to the group. I divide them into two categories. The first, *policy* wins, are outcomes in which the Caucus's tactics are connected to the enactment of desired legislation or the successful blockade or defeat of undesired legislation (i.e., negative agenda-setting power), contrary to the preferences of party leaders. (A policy win by the Caucus is labelled "partial" if a Caucus-desired bill passes the House but fails to become law, or if a Caucus-blocked bill is nonetheless enacted after a nontrivial length of time.) The second category, *political* wins, include successful efforts by the Caucus to exercise positive agenda-setting power by forcing floor votes on desired proposals, but those proposals do not pass the chamber. Table 2 lists the remaining seven cases in which the Freedom Caucus tried but failed to achieve a desired policy or political outcome.

What explains the Freedom Caucus's success or failure in these 18 instances? A case-by-case analysis reveals that the bloc's influence was contingent upon whether it sought to exercise positive or negative influence on the House's agenda; the group's choice of strategy (including, but not

---

[46] For an alternative approach to determining the policy preferences of the Caucus, see Clarke (n.d.).

[47] Taken from the 2015 and 2016 *CQ Almanacs*.

**Table 1** List of Freedom Caucus Legislative Wins, 114th Congress

| Measure/Issue | Date(s) | Caucus Objective | Tactics | Official Position(s)? | Outcome | Nature of Win |
|---|---|---|---|---|---|---|
| Border security bill | Jan 2015 | defeat | oppose bill | no | bill pulled from floor indefinitely | policy |
| FY16 DHS appropriations (3-week funding) | Feb 2015 | defeat | oppose any bill if it fails to overturn WH immigration order | no | leadership bill failed | policy (partial) |
| FY16 budget resolution | Mar 2015 | allow amendments | negotiate rule that permits votes for budget alternatives | no | votes permitted on alternative, leadership budget passed | political |
| D.C. abortion law disapproval | Apr 2015 | pass | officially support bill | yes | resolution passed, failed to become law | policy (partial) |
| No Child Left Behind reauthorization | Apr – Dec 2015 | allow amendments | oppose bill, insist on rule that allows votes for amendments | no | bill delayed, amendments allowed | political |
| Reauthorization of Export-Import Bank | Apr – Oct 2015 | prevent | officially oppose bill | yes | reauthorization expires in July, renewed in December | policy (partial) |

**Table 1** (cont.)

| Measure/Issue | Date(s) | Caucus Objective | Tactics | Official Position(s)? | Outcome | Nature of Win |
|---|---|---|---|---|---|---|
| Iran nuclear deal repeal | Jul – Sept 2015 | repeal agreement/ delay vote until WH reveals "side deals" | officially oppose agreement, support resolution delaying vote, consider opposing rule | yes | initial resolution pulled, votes on three other measures held | policy (partial) |
| Planned Parenthood funding | Jul – Dec 2015 | prevent | officially support defunding, officially oppose appropriations with PP funding, offer amendment to let states defund PP | yes (three times) | anti-funding bills pass House, but final budget maintains full funding, amendment not in order | policy (partial) |
| FY17 budget resolution | Feb – Mar 2016 | defeat, pass alternative | officially oppose bill if fails to impose additional cuts | yes | bill delayed indefinitely | policy |
| Antiterrorism bill | Jul 2016 | defeat | oppose bill | no | bill delayed indefinitely | policy |
| Impeachment of IRS commissioner | May – Dec 2016 | pass | officially support bill, demand hearings, introduce privileged resolution | yes (three times) | committee hearings and floor vote held, resolution referred to committee | political |

**Table 2** List of Freedom Caucus Legislative Losses, 114th Congress

| Measure/Issue | Date(s) | Caucus Objective | Tactics | Official Position? | Outcome |
|---|---|---|---|---|---|
| FY16 DHS appropriations (longer-term funding) | Mar 2015 | defeat | oppose bill if fails to overturn WH immigration order | no | bill passes |
| Trade Promotion Authority | May – Jun 2015 | pass alternative, change House rules | support bill on condition of changes to bill, new House procedures, end to Export-Import Bank | no | no concessions given, rule narrowly passes, original bill narrowly approved |
| First Amendment Defense Act | Jul 2015 | pass | officially support bill | yes | bill dies in committee |
| FY16 Omnibus appropriations | Oct 2015 | add conservative riders | propose amendments to bill | no | amendments not allowed, desired riders excluded |
| FY17 Financial Services appropriations | Jul 2016 | allow amendments | oppose rule if fails to permit amendments | no | promise (unmet) to permit amendments to future bills |
| Five bills (including the First Amendment Defense Act) | Jul 2016 | pass | officially support bills | yes | bills die in committee |
| FY17 Continuing Resolution (1st) | Sep 2016 | defeat, pass alternative | oppose short-term bill, pass medium-term bill with conservative riders | no | short-term bill passes |

limited to, the use of implicit or explicit threats); and the degree of support that other legislators provided. In the next two parts of this section, I discuss the impact of these factors, looking first at instances of Caucus success, then of Caucus failure.

## 3.2 Explaining Freedom Caucus Success

Table 3 summarizes the key conditions that allowed the Freedom Caucus to earn at least partial wins. For bills and resolutions that the Caucus opposed and that were scheduled to come to the floor for a vote, the group was influential when it could effectively threaten to defeat the bills on the House floor with a cross-party majority. These are the most frequent instances (8 of 11), underscoring the powerful impact of the Freedom Caucus's hardnosed approach to negotiation when it had the potency and credibility to back up its threats. Of the remaining three successes, which involved measures desired by the Freedom

**Table 3**  Reasons for Freedom Caucus Legislative Wins

| Bill/Rule on House Agenda | | Bill/ Rule Not on House Agenda |
| --- | --- | --- |
| *Support from Cross-Party Floor Majority and Threaten to Vote Against* | *Support from Committees/ GOP Leaders* | *No Support from Committees/GOP Leaders and Threaten to Force Floor Vote* |
| Border security bill | DC abortion law disapproval | Impeachment of IRS Commissioner |
| FY16 DHS appropriations (3-week funding) | Reauthorization of Export-Import Bank* | |
| FY16 budget resolution | | |
| No Child Left Behind reauthorization | | |
| Iran nuclear deal repeal | | |
| Planned Parenthood funding | | |
| FY17 budget resolution | | |
| Antiterrorism bill | | |

\* Technically, the Caucus's objective was to prevent a bill from coming to the floor, but the political dynamic – needing support from key party members to alter the status quo – was similar.

Caucus but that were absent from the House's agenda, the group succeeded under one of two conditions: either its efforts were supported by key committee chairs, party leaders, or both; or the group lacked that support but could effectively threaten to force a floor vote with a nonmajoritarian procedural mechanism.

*Effective threat to defeat bill or resolution.* The first instance of Caucus policy success occurred on a *border security bill.* Seeking to fulfill a GOP promise for the 114th Congress, Homeland Security Committee Chairman Mike McCaul (R-TX) introduced a bill in January 2015 directing the Department of Homeland Security (DHS) to take steps that would seal off the country's borders to illegal immigration. Democrats were strongly opposed to the bill, not least because McCaul had excluded them from the bill-drafting process. But some conservative Republicans were also upset: they wanted to do more to remove illegal immigrants already in the United States, they worried that the measure would give their party cover to keep in place President Obama's November 2014 executive order to stop enforcing immigration laws on certain undocumented residents, and they feared the bill would become a Trojan Horse for bipartisan immigration reform. At the end of January, the bill lacked a majority and was removed from the House calendar, never to return ("House Border Bill Pleases Neither Party"). Though the role of the Freedom Caucus in this outcome is somewhat unclear, Caucus members were among the most outspoken critics of the measure and the speed with which moved through the legislative process; its leadership had surveyed members on where they stood on the bill; and Caucus member Mo Brooks (MO) attested that enough Caucus members opposed the bill to stop it (Foley 2015; Fuller 2015a; Gehrke 2015a; "House Border Bill Pleases Neither Party").

The influence of the Freedom Caucus drew greater scrutiny shortly thereafter as the House struggled to pass a *three-week funding bill for DHS.* When President Obama issued his executive order on immigration, furious Republicans decided to use DHS appropriations as a way of repealing the order. Congress passed a bill in December to fund the agency through late February, by which time GOP leaders planned to enact a longer-term spending measure with language blocking Obama's executive order ("Homeland Bill Takes a Two-Step"). Freedom Caucus members strongly supported that strategy and implicitly threatened to shut down the agency if the Senate and White House did not comply. After the House passed a DHS funding bill in mid-January that would undo Obama's immigration order, Caucus Chairman Jim Jordan warned that while "no one wants a shutdown . . . the plan, as far as I'm concerned, is our bill." In addition, twenty Republicans, including many members of the Caucus, cosigned a letter to the Speaker "warning Boehner not to cave to Democrats" (Fuller 2015a; "Rep. Boehner: House Has 'Done Its Job'"; Wong 2015a).

However, Senate Democrats called House Republicans' bluff and filibustered the bill. Speaker Boehner hoped to "buy more time" with a clean, three-week DHS stopgap funding bill, which he brought to the floor on February 27 (Duncan 2015c). But conservatives resisted, and fifty-two Republicans – including 24 lawmakers who were, or would become, Caucus members – joined all but 12 Democrats to vote against the measure, killing it by a vote of 203 to 224. GOP leaders would eventually pass another DHS funding bill (see below), but the Freedom Caucus's short-term policy victory had sent a strong signal that its members were not afraid to vote against leadership-endorsed bills on the floor it deemed too moderate, and it had the numbers to defeat them. Their opposition also led some of Boehner's allies to start worrying that the Speaker's standing in the Conference was in jeopardy (see section 4).

Shortly after it failed to block passage of a longer-term DHS appropriations bill in March (see below), the Freedom Caucus met to discuss a *budget resolution for fiscal year 2016*. Acknowledging the bloc's newfound reputation for rejecting leadership bills, Budget Committee Chairman Tom Price (R-GA) held a series of confabs with Caucus Chair Jordan and other members of the group. Boehner agreed to the Caucus's request to allow floor votes on several competing budget plans (French and Kim 2015). A majority of the group voted for two proposals: the original plan proposed by Price (which failed 105–319) and an alternative offered by the Republican Study Committee (RSC) (which also failed, 132–294). Jordan had been unable to get the Caucus to endorse the budget plan offered by leadership, but a majority of its members nevertheless did cast ballots for it (the Caucus voting 27 to 11), and it passed narrowly, 219–208. With that as the final package, the Caucus supported the resolution, 32 to 6, which passed 228–199 (Wong 2015b). Not a single Democrat voted for any of the plans.

The Freedom Caucus again exploited its power to defeat bills when the GOP tried to *revise the No Child Left Behind Act*, a controversial law which tied federal funding for schools to student performances on achievement tests. Education and the Workforce Committee Chair John Kline (R-MN) introduced a bill giving more flexibility to states to set education policy and curtailing some federal school funding. But the majority party was split between conservatives, who also wanted the bill to permit school vouchers and dramatically reduce federally imposed requirements on schools, and moderates, who were less enamored with those proposals. Democrats, meanwhile, found Kline's bill too conservative and complained that the measure had been approved without a single committee hearing. Though the Freedom Caucus did not take an official position on the bill, individual Caucus members – enough to make the difference between passage and failure – expressed deep reservations about it. After a day of floor deliberation, with party leaders futilely whipping for votes, the measure was abruptly withdrawn ("Frustrated with 'No Child Left Behind'"; Severns 2015; Wong 2015c). Kline then consulted with Caucus board member Mick Mulvaney (R-SC), and GOP leaders acceded to the demand of Caucus members for a chance to amend the bill (Dumain and Fuller 2015c; Ferrechio 2015; Wong 2015c). When one amendment offered by Freedom Caucus member Matt Salmon (R-AZ) passed on the floor but another did not, Salmon warned that the bill's passage would be "dicey." Still, many of his Caucus colleagues were open to supporting the bill anyway, and with the voting clock kept open, leadership "twisted arms" until the measure narrowly passed, 218–213, with 24 Caucus members voting for it (Dumain and Fuller 2015c).

The *Iran arms agreement* was another issue on which the Freedom Caucus achieved at least partial success through effective threat-making. After the Obama White House negotiated a multilateral agreement in mid-July 2015 to end Iran's nuclear weapons program, Republicans expressed strong doubts that the deal would prevent Iran from developing weapons or sponsoring overseas terrorism. Congress had already enacted a law that maintained U.S. sanctions against Iran for sixty days while it examined the details of any agreement and allowed the legislative branch to keep those sanctions in place with a two-thirds vote in both chambers ("Unable to Block Nuclear Deal with Iran"). On July 30, the Caucus officially opposed the accord and called upon Congress to disapprove the agreement before the sixty-day deadline expired. GOP leaders agreed, and they pressed for a joint resolution to undo it (Dumain 2016), but things grew complicated when news reports suggested that the White House might have made additional, undisclosed deals with Iran as part of the accord. Caucus members argued that the sixty-day clock should not start until such deals were revealed, and they hinted that they might vote against the rule for considering the original joint resolution (DeBonis and Zezima 2015; Fuller 2015g). Deeming the threat credible and knowing few if any Democrats – whom the White House had been lobbying relentlessly – would vote for the rule, GOP leaders pulled the original joint resolution. By that time, enough Senate Democrats had come out in favor of the agreement to ensure it could not be overturned, making any legislative action symbolic. Instead, the GOP leadership "cave[d] to conservatives" by bringing up several other Iran-related measures to provide position-taking opportunities, force Democrats to go on the record, and preserve the right to sue the Administration for concealing details of the agreement (DeBonis and Zezima 2015; Fuller 2015h; Raju 2015).

*Eliminating funding for Planned Parenthood* was one of the Freedom Caucus's longest legislative campaigns of the 114th Congress. In mid-July 2015, secret videos emerged purporting to show a Planned Parenthood executive discussing the sale of fetal tissue to a medical firm. Bill Flores (R-TX), chair of the RSC – which counted a majority of House Republicans as members – urged an investigation into the group, and Diane Black (R-TN) introduced a bill to suspend funding for the organization for one year. The Freedom Caucus took an official binding position that went further, opposing any funding for Planned Parenthood as long as it was under investigation. When no additional legislative action seemed forthcoming, Mick Mulvaney began collecting signatures on a letter pledging that its signatories "cannot and will not support any funding resolution . . . that contains any funding for Planned Parenthood." On September 10, the Caucus voted to endorse this position, and five days later the RSC followed suit, proposing a budget free of abortion-related funding. As Mulvaney declared, "leadership is going to have to choose: do they want it to be a talking point, or do they want to actually do something about it?" ("Abortion Debate Heats Up Again"; Fuller 2015i; Flores 2015; Haberkorn 2015; Kane and Snell 2015).[48]

Meanwhile, GOP leaders expected that an appropriations bill defunding Planned Parenthood would die in the Senate or be vetoed by the president, leading to a government shutdown that voters could blame on congressional Republicans (Fram and Taylor 2015; Kane and Snell 2015). Leadership brought Black's bill to the floor on September 18, which passed on a near-perfect party line vote in mid-September (241–187), but the Freedom Caucus insisted on using the appropriations process to end Planned Parenthood funding, and the list of signatories on Mulvaney's letter grew to over 30, enough to jeopardize passage of any future appropriations bill without Democratic votes and effectively blocking all GOP spending bills from coming to the floor (Fram and Taylor 2015; "Abortion Debate Heats Up Again"). It was during this standoff that Speaker Boehner announced his early retirement from Congress (see section 4), whereupon he worked with Democrats to pass a Senate-approved funding bill on September 30 that did not cut Planned Parenthood funding. Boehner then successfully negotiated a final budget agreement that maintained funding for Planned Parenthood. The Caucus formally opposed the agreement and voted against it unanimously, but it passed in October with

---

[48] The letter would eventually be signed by 38 Republicans in total, of whom 26 were members of the Caucus (Shabad 2015). The Caucus's position was not universally accepted within the group, and it led one member, Tom McClintock (R-CA), to resign; see section 5.

mostly Democratic votes (Bolton 2015; Bolton and Ferris 2015). Additional legislative proposals supported by the bloc to defund Planned Parenthood were either vetoed by President Obama or not permitted to come to the floor for a vote (see below) ("Abortion Debate Heats Up Again"; French 2015e; P. Sullivan 2015a, 2015b).

Freedom Caucus members and other House conservatives unhappy with the budget agreement that Boehner had negotiated with Democrats latched onto *the next fiscal year's budget resolution* as an opportunity to curtail domestic nonmilitary spending. Caucus Republicans wanted the resolution to set domestic spending limits below the budget agreement's spending caps.[49] Speaker Ryan had an "intense" and ultimately unsuccessful meeting with the group in early February to try to assuage their concerns (Fuller 2016a). Budget Committee Chairman Price eventually offered to allow a vote on a separate budget with $30 billion more in spending cuts, a key demand of the Caucus. However, the bloc approved a binding resolution officially opposing the bill (French 2016; "House Freedom Caucus Helps Define"; McPherson 2016). When Price's committee went ahead and approved a more-generous budget resolution, some Freedom Caucus members insisted they did not unconditionally oppose the resolution, and they offered legislative alternatives that they believed had a realistic chance of becoming law (Cottle 2016a). But none were deemed by Ryan or Price likely to win a floor majority or be an improvement over the status quo, and GOP leaders abandoned the idea of passing a resolution that year (Ferris 2016b).

Finally, the Caucus effectively threatened to keep an *antiterrorism bill* from the House floor. Following a mass shooting in an Orlando nightclub in June 2016, Republican leaders decided to move forward on a bill that would halt gun purchases by suspected terrorists and create an office in DHS to address Islamic "radicalization" (Bade 2016b). Minority party Democrats criticized the bill for imposing weak gun restrictions, while some Republicans expressed alarm that it would strengthen federal limits on individual gun rights while rewarding Democrats who had conducted a high-profile floor protest against gun violence. Facing resistance from conservatives, GOP leaders decided to postpone the vote until it could be discussed in a party-wide meeting, but the meeting was pre-empted when the Freedom Caucus, whose members had been denied the chance to offer amendments to the measure, officially opposed it, and it ultimately never came to the floor (Bade 2016b; Bade and Bresnahan 2016; Friedman 2016).

---

[49] The RSC would also come out against the higher spending caps in late February (Ferris 2016a).

*Support from key committees or party leaders.* The Freedom Caucus some-times wanted to bring a measure to the House floor, not revise or block one scheduled for a vote. In those situations, a persuasive threat to kill legislation or a procedural motion would be of no help, and the Caucus was too small to command a majority in the party or the chamber to exercise positive agenda control. One alternative, which the Caucus employed twice in the 114th Congress, was to leverage support from committee chairs and GOP leaders who *could* shape the agenda.

The Freedom Caucus first followed this path on behalf of a *resolution disapproving Washington, D.C.'s abortion law.* Federal statute gave Congress the authority to overturn any law in the District of Columbia within 30 days of its submission to Congress. In mid-April 2015, Diane Black introduced a resolution striking down a D.C. law that prohibited the punishment of employees for using contraception or having an abortion. The House Oversight Committee, where Caucus members held almost a majority of Republican seats (see section 2), approved the measure on April 21, and eight days later the Caucus endorsed the resolution and urged its consideration on the House floor. Though most House Republicans were pro-life, GOP leaders had been reluctant to schedule a vote on Black's resolution, given the Senate was unlikely to approve the measure in time and the Obama White House would certainly not sign it. But the Caucus's push for the measure was backed up by other party conservatives, most notably RSC Chair Bill Flores, and together with pressure from outside advocacy groups the Caucus convinced Republican leaders to reverse course. The House passed the bill on April 30 on a mostly party-line vote, 228–192, but it did not become law (Bowman 2015; Davis 2015; French 2015a; Fuller 2015e).

The other instance of the Freedom Caucus effectively leveraging support from well-placed allies in Congress involved *reauthorization of the Export-Import Bank.* Funding for the Bank was scheduled to expire at the end of June 2015. Some conservatives, Caucus members among them, saw the Bank as a taxpayer-subsidized intrusion into the free market, and the group's leaders announced at a May press conference that the Caucus officially opposed its reauthorization. Joining Caucus Chair Jordan at the press event was a powerful ally: Financial Services Chairman Jeb Hensarling (R-TX), a long-time Bank opponent whose committee had jurisdiction over reauthorization (Berman 2014). In addition, though Speaker Boehner may have preferred to reform the Export-Import Bank rather than abolish it, other GOP leaders were opposed to letting the Bank continue, and they were joined by such anti-Bank allies as the conservative group Heritage Action and the leadership of the RSC

(Cirilli 2015; Fuller 2015b; Warmbrodt, Sherman, and Guida 2015).[50] With so many well-placed allies and an ability to achieve its objective through congressional inaction, the Caucus successfully saw the Bank's authorization expire at the end of June.

Unfortunately for the Freedom Caucus, a majority of the House preferred reauthorizing the Export-Import Bank. Amid an environment of uncertainty following Speaker Boehner's unexpected resignation in the fall, Bank advocate Stephen Fincher (R-TN) filed a discharge petition to force a reauthorization bill from Hensarling's committee, and it was quickly signed by most Democrats and enough Republicans to receive the requisite 218 signatures.[51] An infuriated Hensarling warned that "signing a discharge petition effectively makes [Minority Leader] Nancy Pelosi the Speaker of the House" (Ho and Snell 2015).[52] But on October 27, the House passed reauthorization by a wide margin, 313–118, with support from majorities of both parties, albeit not from a majority of the Freedom Caucus (Kane 2015). Bank funding was later folded into a transportation bill that passed the House in early November, after the chamber rejected multiple floor amendments from Caucus members (and others) that would restrict the Bank's funding and operations, including one offered by Mick Mulvaney (R-SC) to effectively kill the Export-Import Bank (and rejected by a narrow majority of Republicans). The final bill was signed into law in December 2015.

*Persuasive threat to force a floor vote.* The final instance of a (partial) victory by the Freedom Caucus in the 114th Congress involved issuing a credible threat of a different sort than killing a proposal: forcing the House to consider a bill or resolution through procedural legerdemain. Here, bloc size and unity were less salient sources of threat potency than the opportunity to exploit chamber rules that allowed a minority to shape the agenda – specifically, compelling debate on *impeaching the commissioner of the Internal Revenue Service.*

The impeachment effort originated with a 2013 news report that the IRS had given additional scrutiny to the tax returns of nonprofit groups with conservative-sounding names. Over the next two years, both Congress and the Justice Department conducted investigations, key IRS data disappeared, and Republicans insisted that IRS Commissioner John Koskinen had given

---

[50] RSC opposition notwithstanding, up to one-third of its members had publicly supported reauthorization in the past (Cirilli 2015).

[51] See http://clerk.house.gov/114/lrc/pd/petitions/DisPet0002.xml. Democrats had previously submitted a discharge petition to bring reauthorization to the floor, which garnered 181 signatures (Petition #1, http://clerk.house.gov/114/lrc/pd/petitions/DisPet0001.xml).

[52] Ironically, the same criticism was made of the Freedom Caucus's numerous successful efforts to block majority party leaders by joining with Pelosi's party on the House floor. See section 5.

misleading testimony to Congress. In late October 2015, House Oversight Committee Chairman Jason Chaffetz (R-UT) introduced articles of impeachment against Koskinen with 18 Republican cosponsors, all from his committee and half of them from the Freedom Caucus (Rein 2015). GOP leaders were hardly enamored with impeachment, however: it was unlikely to marshal the required supermajority in the Senate, and it threatened to distract from the party's legislative agenda and presidential campaign (Cottle 2016b). That fewer than half the GOP would eventually cosponsor Chaffetz's resolution suggested the Conference did not want to pursue impeachment either.

As the Judiciary Committee sat on Chaffetz's measure, frustrated members of the Freedom Caucus decided to press the matter further. In early May 2016, after meeting with fellow Caucus members, Jordan and Meadows confronted Speaker Ryan with a threat to force a floor vote on impeachment via a privileged resolution, which could be brought to the floor by a single legislator, unless the Judiciary Committee began taking steps to remove Koskinen. The Committee announced two hearings on the commissioner shortly thereafter (Bade 2016a), but the Caucus was not satisfied. On June 22, the group formally committed to a floor vote on impeachment, and three weeks later, two Caucus members, John Fleming (R-LA) and Tim Huelskamp (R-KS), introduced their own articles of impeachment that were formally endorsed by the Freedom Caucus. On September 13, Fleming (joined on the floor by Huelskamp) announced his intent to introduce a privileged resolution that would force impeachment to the House floor for debate, and the Freedom Caucus voted the same day to support that move (Ota 2016). They subsequently called off their threat when Judiciary Chairman Goodlatte, following a discussion with Jordan, agreed to force Koskinen to testify under oath in his committee (Bade 2016c; Wegmann 2016b).

Finally, after the November elections, with no further action from Goodlatte forthcoming, Jordan introduced a privileged resolution to force consideration of the Fleming-Huelskamp impeachment articles. Republicans immediately rejected a Democratic motion to table the resolution, but Goodlatte promptly moved to refer the articles to his committee for further consideration, and the House concurred, 342–72, with all but three Freedom Caucus members voting against Goodlatte's motion (Jagoda 2016). The Caucus had successfully, if belatedly, forced the full House to consider impeaching Koskinen, though he remained in his post.

## 3.3 Explaining Freedom Caucus Failure

The same variables that contributed to the Freedom Caucus's legislative successes also explain its failures (see Table 4). When a bill or rule was on the

**Table 4** Reasons for Freedom Caucus Legislative Losses

| Bill/Rule on House Agenda | | Bill/Rule Not on House Agenda |
|---|---|---|
| *Threaten to Vote Against and No Support from Cross-Party Floor Majority* | *Do Not Threaten (or Maintain Threat) to Vote Against* | *Unable to Threaten to Force Floor Vote and No Support from Committees/GOP Leaders* |
| FY16 DHS appropriations (longer-term funding) | FY17 Financial Services appropriations | First Amendment Defense Act |
| Trade Promotion Authority | FY17 Continuing Resolution (1st) | Five bills (including the First Amendment Defense Act) |
| FY16 Omnibus appropriations | | |

legislative agenda, the Freedom Caucus was unable to influence outcomes if the group's threats either lacked potency – because the Caucus could not muster a cross-party majority to kill a measure – or were withdrawn. When a bill or rule was not on the agenda, Caucus failure followed when the group could neither get support from influential members of Congress nor use a nonmajoritarian procedural motion to force a floor vote.

*Ineffective threat to defeat bill or resolution.* The first instance of the Caucus being unable to marshal a majority on the floor to back up a threat to defeat a bill was over a *longer-term DHS funding bill*. After Boehner's three-week appropriations bill for the agency was unexpectedly defeated in late February 2015 (discussed above), Freedom Caucus Chair Jordan insisted on a "firmer commitment" to limit Obama's executive order on immigration before he or his colleagues would vote for any other DHS spending bill (S. Sullivan 2015b). There was no hope for Senate passage of a DHS bill containing such a commitment, and House leaders did not want to risk shutting down the Department for lack of funds. Boehner tried to convince his rank-and-file to unify behind him, but conservatives stood firm. Leadership allies tried a more aggressive approach: a political action committee affiliated with GOP leaders funded pro-DHS advertisements in the districts of bill opponents. But the ads only succeeded in alienating Caucus members (Lizza 2015). Nonetheless, the group could not keep Boehner from reaching a deal with House Democrats, and on March 3, over the objection of GOP conservatives, the House voted to concur with the Senate's funding bill, which did not overturn Obama's executive order. Caucus member John Fleming (R-LA) warned, however, that "there are more battles coming" (Sherman and Bresnahan 2015b; S. Sullivan 2015a).

The second instance in which Republican leaders joined forces with members of the minority party to rob Caucus threats of their potency came up during a heated battle over *Trade Promotion Authority* (TPA), the statutory authority of the House and Senate to approve trade agreements with simple majority votes (versus a supermajority vote in just the Senate, as laid out in the Constitution). Obama pressed Congress in early 2015 to pass TPA in anticipation of new trade deals with European and Asian nations, and the president had good reason to think that the traditionally pro–free-trade GOP would agree. The Democratic Party, by contrast, was increasingly opposed to new trade agreements, especially without economic aid programs for displaced U.S. workers, also known as trade adjustment assistance (TAA), something Republicans were less enamored with (Karol 2009; Palmer and Behsudi 2015).

Republican leaders agreed to renew TPA, but in question was whether they would try to pass TPA without TAA, relying on GOP votes alone, or whether they would pair TPA and TAA together, winning Democratic votes but losing Republicans in the process. Some influential Freedom Caucus members stated that their support for any trade authority bill was contingent on three conditions: keeping TPA and TAA separate, creating a procedural mechanism for legislators to vote more easily against trade agreements, and letting the Export-Import Bank's charter expire (see above) (Dennis 2015; French 2015b).[53] Unwilling or unable to meet those terms, the GOP turned to pro-trade Democrats to make up the loss of votes from the Freedom Caucus, permitting consideration of both TAA and TPA. The final bill was brought to the floor in June under a rule that employed a "division of the question" procedure, whereby the House would vote separately on the TPA and TAA provisions and both would have to win majorities in order for the bill to pass ("Congress Grants President Fast-Track Authority for Trade Deals"; Snell 2015).

Disappointed that Boehner had made a deal with Democrats and that the procedural rule undid a provision that had reduced Medicare spending to pay for TAA while allowing lawmakers to avoid going on the record in favor of the

---

[53] Freedom Caucus members added the third condition after Senate GOP leader Mitch McConnell (R-KY) offered to include renewal of the Bank charter in the TPA in exchange for votes for the trade agreement.

Medicare cuts, 28 Caucus members voted against the rule. But eight Democrats voted for it, and after last-minute whipping by GOP leaders, the rule narrowly passed, 217–212 (Buck 2017; Dumain and Fuller 2015a). Matters grew complicated when anti–free-trade Democrats then voted strategically against TAA, hoping to kill TPA, and were joined by enough Republicans to defeat the TAA legislation. A subsequent series of legislative maneuvers overcame that roadblock, and both TPA and TAA passed the House ("Congress Grants President Fast-Track Authority"). Jordan complained that "the Democrats basically got to amend the process; we didn't," but rattled Republican leaders imposed a series of punishments on Caucus members who had voted against the rule, contributing to the eventual downfall of the Speaker of the House (see section 4). Their opposition had also cemented the group's threat credibility. Warned one member of the Caucus, "If Jim Jordan says he has the vote, they have to believe him" (Gehrke 2015b).

The third instance of Freedom Caucus failure due to an impotent threat was over a *fiscal year 2016 omnibus appropriations bill* considered in late 2015. Frustrated that the bill would increase federal spending and not cut off funds to Planned Parenthood (see above), the Caucus at least wanted to offer amendments to the measure that would, among other things, allow states to deny Medicaid payments to Planned Parenthood, slash funding for certain environmental regulations, and tighten restrictions on the admittance of Iraqi and Syrian refugees (P. Sullivan 2015a; Wong 2015f). The GOP leadership believed that any potential poison pill amendments to an appropriations bill would lead to a government shutdown, a view that remained unchanged even after Boehner was replaced as Speaker by Paul Ryan. The leadership-dominated Rules Committee allowed none of the Caucus's amendments, and dismayed members of the group vowed to oppose the bill, a threat that all but four carried out. Their opposition meant little, though, as Ryan and Pelosi had negotiated the details of the omnibus spending measure, and majorities of both parties cast ballots in favor of it (Sherman, French, and Palmer 2015; Wong 2015f).

*Failing to threaten (or maintain a threat) to vote against a measure.* On two occasions, the Freedom Caucus backed away from its initial threats to oppose legislation, accepting nothing (or nearly nothing) in exchange. One was over consideration of a *Financial Services appropriations bill*, which funded the Treasury Department, the federal court system, and other agencies. In July 2016, as the House prepared to consider the bill, members of the Caucus complained that two potential amendments related to gun ownership written by Caucus ally Thomas Massie (R-KY) had not been made in order. Without concessions from leadership, Raúl Labrador warned, "the rule was going down" (Fuller 2016b). Speaker Ryan responded that Massie's amendments would be toxic, given a recent gun massacre at an Orlando nightclub, and instead suggested that they could be considered separately in committee (Fuller 2016b), an (ultimately unmet) promise that apparently satisfied the group enough for it to end its threat.

The other instance involved the *first fiscal year 2017 continuing resolution* spending bill. With a September 30 deadline to pass appropriations bills looming on the horizon, GOP leaders wanted to enact a short-term spending measure, buying more time to complete negotiations with the Senate and White House on funding the government through 2017. But in a full Conference meeting, Jim Jordan and other like-minded Republicans advocated for a longer-term bill to avoid a lame-duck Congress setting budget policy – or, at the very least, including desired policy riders in the spending bill, such as a halt on admitting refugees from Syria (Bade and Weyl 2016). Ignoring the Caucus chair's pleas, the leadership reached an agreement with Democrats on a short-term spending bill that lacked conservative policy riders. The Freedom Caucus chose not to press the point, and the measure passed the House by a wide margin, 342–85, with majorities of both parties (including 12 Caucus members) voting in favor (Huetteman 2016).

*Inability to threaten a floor vote and lacking support from key committees or party leaders.* Finally, two sets of Freedom Caucus–backed measures remained off the legislative agenda in the 114th Congress because the group had neither support from powerful allies in Congress nor an available procedural mechanism to force the measures onto the House agenda. The first involved a bill introduced while the Supreme Court deliberated over whether state prohibitions on gay marriage were unconstitutional. Social conservatives rallied behind tradition-minded business owners, ministers, and others who declared that their religious convictions kept them from offering marriage-related services to same-sex couples. In June 2015, Caucus member Raúl Labrador introduced the *First Amendment Defense Act*, which would guarantee protection from government sanction for those who were opposed to gay marriage, and the group formally endorsed the bill in early July. But while the measure would garner the RSC's endorsement as well, plus cosponsors from a majority of the Conference, neither GOP leaders nor the chair of Ways and Means, one of the committees to which the bill had been referred, expressed much interest in putting gay marriage on the legislative agenda (DeBonis 2015a). The same problem would hinder another *four bills introduced by Freedom Caucus members*, which the bloc formally endorsed as a group in July 2016 (along with the First Amendment

Defense Act, for a second time).[54] None of the bills saw any legislative action in the 114th Congress.

## 3.4 Discussion and Conclusion

The foregoing analysis revealed that the Freedom Caucus achieved some degree of success in shaping outcomes. In most cases, hard bargaining tactics were employed by the Caucus, including threats, though those threats were sometimes made obliquely or implicitly. When the group sought to alter or defeat measures that were already on the agenda, two key factors mattered: whether the Caucus threatened to vote against leadership-desired bills, and if those threats were potent (i.e., a cross-party majority of the House would support the Caucus and defeat the measure). When the bloc sought to bring up measures that were not yet on the agenda, negative threats were of no use, and as Caucus member Mick Mulvaney later recalled, "we never had the votes in the Freedom Caucus to dictate our own legislation" (Dumain 2017). But the group still found success when it had support from key committee chairs and/or party leaders, or if it could persuasively threaten to follow a nonmajoritarian procedural route that forced bills onto the floor.[55]

The evidence is also consistent with the theoretical reasons outlined in section 1 for why an ideological bloc from the far wing of its party might employ hard bargaining with its own leadership, even at the risk of defeating proposals closer to its policy preferences. In many cases, the Freedom Caucus insisted that the underlying legislation was too distant from the Caucus median member and should be rejected. Sometimes the proposal was identical to the status quo, such as appropriations bills that maintained existing funding for Planned Parenthood, or it moved policy further to the left, such as the antiterrorism bill. Some proposals promised a rightward shift in policy, yet were deemed by the Caucus to be no better than the status quo in either content or effect, such as with the border security bill (which lacked language on deportation and Obama's executive order on immigration), the No Child Left Behind reauthorization (which did not deregulate schools enough), and the FY17 budget resolution (which did not impose greater spending cuts). In some instances, the group (also) had incentives to challenge majority party leaders

---

[54] They included a measure to prohibit discrimination against antiabortion health care providers (H.R. 4828), a bill requiring agency revenue from fees or settlements to deposit the revenue in the general Treasury (H.R. 5499), a bill to block refugees (H.R. 3314), and a measure instituting various reforms to federal welfare programs (H.R. 5360).

[55] Other intraparty organizations have followed a similar strategy when they lacked the ability to reverse floor votes, such as the Southern bloc of House Democrats in the 1930s through 1950s (Rubin 2017).

for electoral or influence-related objectives. For example, the Caucus complained that it was excluded from the bill-writing or amendment process for the antiterrorism bill, Trade Promotion Authority, and the Financial Services bill. Strongly held attitudes among Republican and conservative voters also corresponded with some instances of Freedom Caucus challenges to leadership. Surveys found majorities of Republicans wanted to block Obama's executive order on immigration, even at the risk of shutting down the government; regarded the Iran nuclear deal as unacceptable; and endorsed a government shutdown to defund Planned Parenthood.[56]

Some additional observations about the Caucus follow from the foregoing analysis. First, and perhaps most importantly, the group was far more successful at positive agenda control (i.e., political victories, which happened three times) and negative agenda control (i.e., permanently blocking legislative proposals, which happened another three times) than at other kinds of influence. All other outcomes deemed legislative successes were short-term or partial; in no case in the 114th Congress did the group get a desired bill enacted into law; and just once did it change the policy status quo – ending reauthorization for the Export-Import Bank – a change that only lasted for several months. Furthermore, of the Caucus's seven failures, all but one, the FY17 Financial Services appropriations bill, were efforts at a policy victory versus a political one. This lack of policy enactments (plus deals made between GOP leaders and Democrats to pass more-moderate legislation, like the second DHS funding bill or appropriations for Planned Parenthood, in order to circumvent Caucus opposition) may have been a source of frustration for the group (Bade 2016e). More generally, it suggests there are important limitations to using hard-nosed bargaining tactics in the legislative setting.

Second, the number of Republicans who voted along Caucus lines on the three-week DHS funding bill (52) and the IRS commissioner impeachment resolution (72) exceeded the size of the group, suggesting the veracity of insiders' claims (quoted in the previous section) that there were a decent number of non-Caucus affiliates members willing to join it on floor votes, giving the group greater pivotal power. Third, the Freedom Caucus's binding rule was an important, but by no means determinative, precondition for success. Though the group achieved at least a partial victory for six of the eight measures on which it took at least one formal binding position, it also demonstrated influence in five instances where it took no formal position, and taking a formal position did not prevent several instances of Caucus defections

---

[56] ABC News/Washington Post, January 12–15, 2015 [USABCWP.011915.R19]; Fram and Swanson 2015; Kull and Gallagher 2015.

in floor votes.[57] Fourth, the sequence and overlapping nature of events likely had an impact on the behavior and influence of the Caucus. When the bloc carried out threats early in 2015, for instance, it likely increased its threat credibility in subsequent negotiations. Some disputes arose simultaneously, perhaps giving party leaders an incentive to cooperate with the group on some issues in the hopes of placating them on others. For instance, the decision to delay (indefinitely) the disapproval vote on the Iran agreement may have been taken to defuse conflict between the Caucus and GOP leaders over Planned Parenthood funding (Fuller 2015h).

Finally, the analysis in this section has been necessarily limited to observed instances of Freedom Caucus influence on legislative and procedural measures, and I have excluded public positions on non-House and/or nonlegislative matters. The most significant example of the latter occurred when the Caucus made a major play to remove Speaker John Boehner from office in 2015, which I turn to next.

## 4 Threat-Making and Leadership Selection

We have seen how the House Freedom Caucus found some degree of political success, if not policy success, during its first two years by using hard bargaining tactics with GOP leaders on bills and procedural motions. But what role did these tactics play in perhaps its greatest political win, pushing John Boehner out of the Speakership?[58] Threats by factions against a party's policy-making or agenda-setting authority are one thing, but successfully removing the Speaker of the House is quite another. Not only is it extremely rare for a group to even attempt it, but incumbent leaders have substantial advantages that protect them from intraparty revolts. Yet the example of the Freedom Caucus suggests that party extremists can effectively employ threats to topple their own party's leaders.

In this section, I examine the circumstances surrounding Boehner's retirement and replacement in the 114th Congress. I argue that while a credible threat by the Freedom Caucus almost certainly nudged Boehner from power, it took some time for the group's members to rally behind the tactic, and the influence of the Caucus was contingent upon Boehner's own desire to be Speaker and his distaste for holding a vote to stay in office. In addition, while some gave the

---

[57] These include votes to reauthorize the Export-Import Bank (8 defections), pass a fiscal year 2016 budget with Planned Parenthood funding (4 defections), and the motion to refer impeachment of the IRS Commissioner to committee (3 defections).

[58] Of the first 100 most relevant news stories about the Freedom Caucus in 2015 that appeared in a Lexis-Nexis search, the most frequent (22) were about Boehner's resignation and the selection of his successor.

Caucus credit for exercising veto power over who would replace Boehner, that power was limited, and the group could do little to keep Paul Ryan from becoming his successor.

## 4.1 The Selection and Tenure of Speakers of the House

Unlike other party leaders in Congress, the Speaker of the House is subject to two votes: a nomination vote within his party and a vote of the full House. In addition, the Speaker can be removed if a majority of the chamber approves a privileged floor motion known as a motion to vacate the chair. Despite this additional selection hurdle, and the ability for its occupant to be removed mid-Congress, the Speakership is usually a highly desirable post. It is the only leadership officer of the House explicitly named in the Constitution, and it has substantial formal and informal powers that make the job appealing and provide leverage over would-be challengers. Thus, once elected, Speakers are usually sufficiently satisfied and secure in their post to remain as long as they stay in Congress and their party is in the majority (Green and Harris 2019; Jenkins and Stewart 2013).

Nonetheless, by the time the House Freedom Caucus had emerged onto the political scene, the careers of Speakers had become less stable. Before the mid-1980s, Speakers usually ended their careers by retiring at the end of a Congress or dying in office. But starting in 1989, every Speaker either lost re-election to the House [Tom Foley (D-WA)], lost the post because the opposing party won control of the chamber [Dennis Hastert (R-IL) and Nancy Pelosi (D-CA)], or in the case of two Speakers, Jim Wright (D-TX) and Newt Gingrich (R-GA), resigned midterm. The norm of strict allegiance to the nominee of one's party had also begun to erode. In 1997, a faction of congressional Republicans plotted to remove Speaker Gingrich with a motion to vacate the chair, and in 2013 and 2015, multiple Republicans voted against Boehner for Speaker on the House floor (Green and Bee 2016). Though the attempted coup against Gingrich unraveled before it could be implemented, it established a procedural path that the Freedom Caucus would threaten to follow against Boehner nearly two decades later.

## 4.2 Explaining Boehner's Resignation

As noted in section 2, Boehner had struggled to manage the more rebellious members of his party ever since becoming speaker in 2010. At first, he resisted using punishment to corral wayward Republicans (Draper 2012; Kane and Fahrenthold 2013), but over time Boehner increasingly resorted to using the stick over the carrot. Four lawmakers deemed insufficiently loyal were stripped of choice committee assignments in late 2012. Later, Boehner removed two future Caucus members from the prestigious Rules Committee when they voted against him for speaker in January 2015, and a third, Rod Blum (R-IA), was excluded from the party's list of vulnerable candidates eligible for campaign help (Cahn 2015; Green and Bee 2016; Sherman and Bresnahan 2015a). "Voting against the Speaker flips a switch," Caucus member Dave Brat (R-VA) later said. "You don't get on any good committees, you don't get on the money committees, you don't get money. The leadership shuts you off from PAC funding, and so on" (Lizza 2015). In February 2015, committee chairs warned the heads of their subcommittees that they must vote with the party on the floor, and two Republican whips who were (or would soon become) Freedom Caucus members, Ron DeSantis (FL) and Jeff Duncan (SC), quit after being told that their leadership posts were conditional on voting for majority-party procedural motions (French and Palmer 2015a; French and Sherman 2015).

Members of the Caucus chafed at these crackdowns, and it did not take long for rumors to swirl that more than Boehner's policy majorities in the House might be in danger. When the first DHS funding measure was defeated in late February 2015, the Speaker's allies feared that he could be subject to a floor motion to vacate the chair that would remove him from the Speakership (DeBonis and Kane 2015). After an outside group allied with leadership began running negative campaign ads against Caucus members, hoping to pressure them into voting for a longer-term DHS appropriations bill, they became even more estranged from party leaders. "Once you attack us in our home districts, there's really no going back from that," Caucus member Mark Meadows later said. "You can't walk into a meeting and say, 'Let's all be on the same team' while at the same moment you're attacking members of the team. It was the beginning of the end" (Lizza 2015).

More punishments by leadership followed the near-defeat of the rule for considering Trade Promotion Authority in June 2015. Boehner warned that "voting against rules is not a vote of conscience; it is a vote to hand the floor over to [Minority Leader] Nancy Pelosi" (Sherman and Palmer 2015a). Three of the 28 Freedom Caucus members who had voted against the rule were either removed or pre-emptively resigned from their whip positions, and Meadows was briefly stripped of his Oversight subcommittee chairmanship before other committee members from the Caucus forced his reinstatement (Fuller 2015d; Wong 2015d).[59] These punishments further created what one former

---

[59] Meadows also complained that he was subject to other sanctions, such as denial of opportunities to conduct official travel (Dumain and Fuller 2015a).

congressional staffer described as a "gulag archipelago" of disgruntled conservatives (Lochhead 2015).

On July 28, Meadows introduced a privileged resolution to declare the speakership vacant, citing excessive centralization of decision-making power within the Conference and the capricious punishment of dissenters (Lizza 2015). Though Meadows was a board member of the Freedom Caucus, his move caught Chairman Jordan and other Caucus members off-guard, and for a time it was unclear how many from the group would endorse it. By mid-September the showdown between the Caucus and Boehner over funding for Planned Parenthood was reaching a crescendo, and with no obvious way out for the Speaker, a government shutdown seemed a very real possibility. Then, on September 25, Boehner unexpectedly announced his early retirement.

Most initial news accounts attributed full responsibility for Boehner's resignation to the Freedom Caucus for threatening to remove him from leadership via the privileged resolution. However, careful consideration of available evidence suggests that the Caucus's threat to remove Boehner was not as potent as widely believed. The mere presence of the motion, as Devin Nunes (R-CA) later claimed, "hung 'like a sword' over Boehner's head" (House 2016), but many Caucus Republicans opposed Meadows's resolution initially, and fellow members of the board even tried to stop Meadows from filing it (Bade 2016c; French 2015d; Fuller 2015m). It did not become credible until a few months later, when Caucus members grew exasperated with Boehner and his unwillingness to use the appropriations process to defund Planned Parenthood. At a meeting between Boehner, Jordan, and four other members of the group the day before Boehner's announced departure, Raúl Labrador told Boehner he should resign if he were unwilling to "change the way you're running this place" (Lizza 2015). Yet it was never clear that many Republicans would vote for the privileged resolution, and Minority Leader Nancy Pelosi (D-CA) had privately assured Boehner that enough Democrats would vote "present" to defeat it (Alberta 2017b).

What did make the Caucus's threat potent was that a vote to vacate the chair was privileged and therefore, under House rules, it could not be blocked. Boehner had calculated that making the GOP rank-and-file go on the record over whether to keep him as Speaker would be politically hazardous to them, because he was unpopular with voters, especially Republicans. Surveys that year showed that respondents who were unfavorable to Boehner outnumbered those who were favorable, with anywhere from a 13 to a 32 percentage point difference between the two groups, and the percent of Republicans with positive perceptions of Boehner had fallen from 54 percent in April 2014 to

37 percent the following August.[60] Another survey taken just before his departure found that, among Republican primary voters who had an opinion on the matter, twice as many wanted Boehner (along with Senate Majority Leader Mitch McConnell) "removed immediately from their leadership position."[61] It was thus a "frustrated" Boehner who privately told Greg Walden (R-OR) that the motion "put[s] Republicans in a tough position to have to make that vote to have to defend him" (Lizza 2015).[62] Meanwhile, Boehner had already lost interest in the job and had even considered retiring at the end of the previous Congress. In a press conference after he announced his retirement, he insisted he was confident he would win on the floor, but "I don't want to put my colleagues through this … for what?" Finally, Boehner may have hoped that, by becoming a lame-duck Speaker, he could more easily negotiate with Democrats on appropriations bills to avoid a government shutdown, as proved to the be the case (Alberta 2017b; Siddiqui, Jacobs, and McCarthy 2015; Wehrman 2015).

In short, the Freedom Caucus's threat only gradually became credible, and when it did, its potency was based not on its passage but on its consideration. Boehner was also, in retrospect, a soft target for the Caucus. Threat-making did work in this case, but only because the incumbent leader was uniquely vulnerable.

## 4.3 Choosing a Successor

Following Boehner's announcement, the Freedom Caucus sought to exploit the impression that it had used its persuasive threat-making power to remove the Speaker. Jordan announced the Caucus had "every intention of voting together as a group" on the selection of Boehner's successor, and other Caucus leaders insisted that Speaker candidates commit to rules changes that would curtail the punishment of dissenters and empower the rank-and-file (Boland 2015; DeBonis 2015b; Fuller 2015k).[63] Majority Leader Kevin McCarthy (R-CA) met with GOP conservatives, including members of the Caucus, at a candidate forum, but the group endorsed Daniel Webster (R-FL), a long-shot alternative,

---

[60] Gallup Polls, April and September 2014, USGALLUP.051514.R03B and USGALLUP.100614. R04B; and Jones 2015.

[61] NBC/Wall Street Poll, September 20–24, 2015, USNBCWSJ.092815.R20. In a survey taken of Republicans after Boehner's announcement, 54 percent believed his departure would be "good for the Republican Party." Pew Research Center poll, September 22–27, 2015, USPSRA.092815.R79.

[62] Lizza (2015) argues that Boehner had decided to resign before his meeting with the Freedom Caucus delegation.

[63] Freedom Caucus members drafted a memo with proposed Conference rule changes and a list of questions for speaker candidates encompassing both conservative policy goals and open procedures and rules changes granting more power to GOP conservatives (Rubin 2017).

and insisted on several procedural changes – including more Caucus representation on influential committees and the party's Steering Committee, more party campaign funding in their districts, and the election of committee chairs by committee members themselves – as the price for their support (French and Palmer 2015b).

The Freedom Caucus's unity soon frayed, however, and its ability to serve as king-maker proved limited. Reid Ribble (R-NJ) became the second member to publicly leave the bloc, complaining it should not have gotten involved in party leadership selection at all (see section 5), and some Caucus members said they would still vote for McCarthy as Speaker (DeBonis 2015b; Dumain 2015b; French and Palmer 2015b; Fuller 2015g). The group's reputation for influence was briefly burnished when McCarthy abruptly ended his candidacy, though it had only endorsed Webster for the Speaker vote in the GOP Conference – where he was almost certain to be outvoted by McCarthy supporters – keeping open the possibility of voting for McCarthy on the House floor (Boland 2015; French and Palmer 2015b).[64] The majority leader's withdrawal created even more chaos and uncertainty in the Conference, and Boehner lobbied Paul Ryan, chair of the Ways and Means Committee and former Vice Presidential candidate, to run instead. When Ryan reluctantly agreed to do so, he deftly exploited his own popularity, his well-known hesitation to be Speaker, and the growing urgency in the GOP to select a viable alternative for Boehner as leverage against the Freedom Caucus. He dutifully met with the group but insisted on its endorsement as a precondition for staying the race, agreeing only in general terms to the procedural changes the group sought (Sherman and French 2015). A sizeable number of Caucus members, enough to block a formal endorsement of Ryan by the group, wanted to honor their commitment to Webster and may have hoped to hold out for more concessions from Ryan. But others, particularly Caucus board members, determined that their bargaining position was weak: failure to support Ryan could lead more lawmakers to exit the organization, and Republicans "would be outraged if 39 members stymied their dream speaker" (Fuller 2015l). Two-thirds of the bloc eventually agreed to "support" Ryan, and after winning the conference election against Webster, 200–43, he received the votes of all but six Freedom Caucus members in the floor vote for Speaker (Sherman and French 2015).

Ryan had outmaneuvered the Freedom Caucus, but he still recognized the wisdom of not repeating Boehner's mistakes. As Speaker he followed a "politics of inclusion" strategy, bringing the Caucus closer to leadership and

---

[64] Some speculated that McCarthy's withdrawal was prompted by a statement from Walter Jones (R-NC) that lawmakers who had committed ethical misconduct should not run for leadership (Sherman 2015).

expanding its members' decision-making authority (Farrell 2001). Freedom Caucus member Tim Huelskamp (KS), who had been booted from the Agriculture Committee by Boehner for disloyalty, was given a subcommittee chairmanship in the Committee of Small Business and elected to one of the newly created at-large positions on the party's Steering Committee (Dumain 2015c; Hawkings 2015). The Speaker created an advisory committee that included Jordan and Mick Mulvaney; opened informal lines of communication with the Caucus via individual meetings with group members, weekly dinners, and personal texts; and provided campaign assistance to members of the group. Even the leadership-allied campaign group, which had once funded ads against Caucus members, began sponsoring positive commercials on their behalf (McPherson 2015; Sherman and Palmer 2015b; Snell 2016).

For a time – perhaps because Ryan was more popular and inclusive than Boehner – the Freedom Caucus tempered its legislative and procedural demands and refrained from holding Ryan responsible for outcomes it disliked. For instance, when the House failed to pass a budget resolution in the spring of 2016, Huelskamp said, "I'm blaming the former speaker. [Ryan] is an heir to the house that John Boehner put together" (Ferris 2016b).[65] But as documented in the previous section, the Caucus still threatened to vote against bills and procedural motions to bring about desired objectives. When Huelskamp lost his primary in the summer of 2016, furious Caucus Republicans blamed Ryan for refusing to reassign him to the Agriculture Committee, and some were further irritated when the Speaker distanced himself from GOP presidential nominee Donald Trump. By the fall of 2016, a number of Caucus members contemplated either voting against Ryan for Speaker, linking their Speaker vote to meaningful rules reforms, or putting Jordan up as a challenger to Ryan.[66] Only after the November elections, which promised a unified Republican government for the next two years, did such discussions dissipate (Alberta 2016b; Bade 2016e; Snell 2016; Wong 2016).

## 4.4 Conclusion

The Freedom Caucus was widely credited with bringing down an incumbent Speaker of the House, a virtually unprecedented feat in the modern Congress.

---

[65] This deference to Ryan may explain why the Caucus backed off from threats to defeat the rule for considering the Financial Services Appropriations bill after being given only vague promises of future opportunities to amend the bill (see previous section).

[66] There was also some discussion of forcing a delay in leadership elections altogether to prevent legislative mischief during the expected lame-duck session and for Caucus members to "make their case" for meaningful rules reforms (Bade 2016d).

But in fact, the Caucus lacked a cross-party coalition to remove Boehner, and its efforts to choose his replacement had little support in the Conference. Instead, it exploited Boehner's unpopularity and the right of any individual member to force a vote on the motion to vacate the chair, while Boehner himself was reluctant to put his colleagues at electoral risk by having to publicly endorse him for a job he no longer wanted. In other words, the group's threat to force a floor vote to retain Boehner was effective insofar as it was credible and the vote itself – not its outcome – imposed sufficient costs to compel Boehner's departure. After that victory, however, the Caucus was divided over the choice of Boehner's replacement, and it lacked enough allies in the Republican Party or among Democrats to effectively threaten a veto over an unfavored candidate, especially one as popular as Paul Ryan.

In the next section, I use the example of the Freedom Caucus to tease out the broader costs and benefits of legislative threat-making. I show that, while the group did gain some additional benefits from its use of effective threats, it also suffered nontrivial harm. Taken together, they paint a mixed picture of the utility of threats in legislative bargaining.

## 5 Other Costs and Benefits of Legislative Threat-Making

The previous sections illustrated the potential influence of congressional threat-making by a bloc of lawmakers in two spheres: legislating and the selection of party leaders. Here, I use the Freedom Caucus as a case study to identify other potential costs and benefits of employing threats in the legislative arena. I find that, while the Caucus and/or its members did reap some political and policy gains from the use of hard-nosed bargaining, the collective and individual harm that was suffered offers a cautionary tale to those who would pursue assertive bargaining techniques against the leadership of one's own political party.

### 5.1 Nonlegislative Costs and Benefits of Threat-Making

I consider four categories of political, nonlegislative costs and benefits that may follow from the use of aggressive bargaining by an intraparty congressional bloc. These include *electoral* benefits (winning elections, raising campaign funds, garnering positive media coverage); *influence-related* benefits (the ability to wield power within the chamber more broadly); the *successful pursuit of higher office* by members of the bloc; and the bloc's success in *maintaining or expanding its size*.

*Electoral.* Because reporters had managed to identify most, if not all, of the Freedom Caucus's members by mid-2015, their constituents could evaluate their incumbent in part by using the group's behavior and reputation as portrayed by the news media. The Caucus regularly issued press releases and made its top leaders available for regular interviews in the press, and the bloc received substantial media attention in the 114th Congress, particularly after the resignation of John Boehner as Speaker (Clarke n.d.). Though it is difficult to gauge the quantity and content of news reporting of the Freedom Caucus in individual congressional districts, much of the national coverage of the group was divided. On the one hand, news stories and op-ed columns commonly ran with critical headlines like "The Freedom Caucus Is Nothing But Cowards" and "Maybe the 'Crazies' in the House GOP Really Are Crazy" (Meyer 2015; Newell 2015). On the other hand, conservative columnists and news outlets countered with positive spins on the group's activities (e.g., Will 2017). In the end, the news media appeared to have minimal impact on voters' perceptions: one survey from early 2017 found that most Americans knew little or nothing of the group, though it was seen favorably among conservatives who were familiar with it (Gramlich 2017).

Caucus membership did not seem to make much of a difference in campaign fundraising either. In the 2016 election cycle, the campaign committees of Republican incumbents running for re-election raised an average (mean) of $1.8 million, nine percent more than they had in 2014. But among those Republicans who were Freedom Caucus members and running for re-election, the average haul was only $1.1 million, 3 percent *less* than they had raised in the previous election cycle.[67] The difference would have likely been even greater had Caucus member Mark Meadows not established a leadership political action committee, the House Freedom Fund, which contributed to the re-election campaigns of several Freedom Caucus members.[68] In fact, the Caucus's independent financial sources and greater reliance on affiliated PACs were strategic responses to its members' exclusion from existing party leadership fundraising networks (Bade and Caygle 2016; Clarke n.d.; McGee 2017; Reynolds and Hall 2019). Meadows himself admitted he was "fired" by his own fundraiser after filing a motion to declare the speakership vacant in mid-2015 (Siegel 2015).

---

[67] This could be because Caucus members were from safer districts. However, Caucus members facing contested elections in 2014 (and who ran for re-election in 2016) won by an average of 65 percent of the two-party vote, slightly below the average margin of victory for all House Republican candidates. In addition, Caucus members who won re-election in 2016 by 60 percent or more of the vote had an average campaign expenditure of $769,000, well below the $1.4 million average expenditure of all GOP incumbents who won with at least 60 percent of the vote.

[68] The group had a second political action committee, the House Freedom Action Fund, that supported the campaigns of incumbents and new candidates (Clarke n.d.).

Finally, empirical data suggest that the impact of Freedom Caucus membership on re-election was largely a wash, and in individual cases may have been politically fatal. Most members of the group who ran for re-election in 2016 were returned to Congress, and 78 percent of Caucus incumbents and two-thirds of first-time Republican candidates given financial contributions by the House Freedom Fund won election that year. However, incumbent Caucus members did no better in winning votes than their non-Caucus counterparts in the GOP Conference: excluding lawmakers unopposed in either election cycle, Caucus members received an average 0.6 percent less of the two-party vote in 2016 than they had in 2014, before the group was formed, compared to an average 0.4 percent less of the vote for non-Caucus incumbent Republicans, a statistically insignificant difference. Meanwhile, for two Freedom Caucus members in particular, the perception of being too conservative and/or obstreperous likely cost them their seats: Tim Huelskamp (R-KS), who lost his primary to a more conventional GOP opponent, and Scott Garrett (R-NJ), who came under fire for his outspoken social conservatism and was defeated by a Democratic challenger. (Two other Caucus members, Rod Blum (R-IA) and Dave Brat (R-VA), lost re-election in November 2018, and a third, Mark Sanford (R-SC), lost his primary earlier that year.)

*Internal influence.* The effect of Freedom Caucus membership in improving lawmakers' internal influence is not clear-cut. As a group, the bloc demonstrated considerable legislative leverage in the 114th Congress, and it arguably expanded its influence after its early victories, acquiring a sort of anticipatory veto power that led lawmakers to seek advance input from the group on the content of legislation. In fact, on at least two occasions party leaders consulted with Caucus leaders or members prior to bringing up major bills (Wong 2015e; Wong and Lane 2016).

Furthermore, over the course of the 114th Congress, Caucus members went from being largely excluded from power to gaining important posts of formal authority. After Speaker Boehner was replaced by Ryan, a representative of the Freedom Caucus was invited to meet regularly with Ryan to discuss upcoming legislative matters, and Conference rules were changed so that it would be possible for the Caucus to elect a representative to the powerful Steering Committee, resulting in Tim Huelskamp's election to the Committee. One Freedom Caucus member, David Schweikert (R-AZ), even gained an assignment to the prestigious Ways and Means Committee in early 2017. Add to that the additional leverage the group could draw upon from issue advocacy groups like FreedomWorks as well as sympathetic Senators like Ted Cruz (R-TX), and the group and its members would seem to have acquired substantial influence by the end of the 114th Congress.

However, the Caucus's power within the party was not as great as it could have been. As explained in the previous section, the Caucus lacked leverage over Ryan when he courted their votes to become Speaker in late 2015, and its dalliance with rules reforms that might have empowered the rank-and-file proved brief. The group could not convince Ryan to reappoint Tim Huelskamp to the Agriculture Committee, which may have contributed to his primary election loss. Even more problematic was that Caucus members had managed to alienate many of their colleagues. The level of private animus held by other Republicans towards members of the group is difficult to gauge, but one survey showed large majorities of congressional staff from both parties had negative views of the Freedom Caucus, while a group of freshmen Republicans were sufficiently upset with freshman class president and Caucus member Ken Buck (R-CO) for defying party leaders on the June trade vote that they threatened to remove him from his post (Cogan 2015; Zeller 2017). Many House members openly violated Ronald Reagan's famous Eleventh Commandment, "Thou shall not speak ill of another Republican," by criticizing the group. A review of news stories about the Caucus during the 114th Congress uncovered multiple GOP members and staff disparaging it:

* "They're not legislators, they're just assholes . . . the craziest of the crazy." – Republican staffer (Fuller 2015a)
* "This is unprecedented to have this small group, a tiny minority, hijack the party and blackmail the House." – Rep. Peter King (R-NY) (Howell 2015)
* "The so-called Freedom Caucus has to figure out if they want to govern or be obstructionists." – Rep. Adam Kinzinger (R-IL) (Howell 2015)
* "The rejectionist arm of the party seems to have a problem with James Madison and the system [of checks and balances] that he devised." – Rep. Charlie Dent (R-PA) (Newton-Small 2015)
* "What have you done that's accomplished anything?" – Rep. Tom Cole (R-OK) to Freedom Caucus member Rep. Mick Mulvaney (R-SC) (Herszenhorn 2015)

Many of the criticisms were rooted in the view that, by defeating Republican bills and procedural motions as part of incidental voting coalitions with Democrats, the Freedom Caucus had helped the minority party. Devin Nunes (R-CA) warned that "when you vote against rules, you hand the House over to Nancy Pelosi" (Disler 2015).

Members of the bloc seemed well aware of the social costs associated with being difficult. Asked why they were willing to oppose party leaders on major bills, one Caucus member told the author, "it's not because you want to be invited to parties, I can tell you that."[69] The bigger problem was that burning bridges with colleagues endangered Caucus members' influence over the long run, since developing alliances with lawmakers and nonlawmakers is one of the key "habits of highly effective lawmakers" (Volden and Wiseman 2014, 188). The impact of this can be hard to gauge. One possible indicator is that lawmakers who joined the Freedom Caucus saw a drop in the average number of cosponsors to their bills, from 18.7 in the 113th Congress to 15.7 in the 114th.[70] A decline in support from colleagues also seemed to manifest itself on two specific occasions. When Speaker Ryan created six at-large elected posts on the Republican Steering Committee, Tim Huelskamp was the only one of four Freedom Caucus members who ran to be selected by his peers (Hawkings 2015). Later, during the 115th Congress, Jim Jordan decided not to run for chair of the House Oversight Committee because the appointment would be made by the party's leadership-aligned Steering Committee, precluding the selection of "guys like me who don't always go along with the establishment" (Marcos 2017).

*Pursuit of higher office.* Freedom Caucus affiliation did not appear to help its members who sought to leave the House for higher elected office, even when they made it a prominent feature of their campaigns. In 2015, two Caucus Republicans, John Fleming (LA) and Marlin Stutzman (IN), ran for open seats in the U.S. Senate. During his campaign, Stutzman emphasized his membership in the Caucus, and he earned financial support and endorsements from various conservative organizations. But he won only a third of the vote and lost to a non-Caucus House member, Todd Young (Kamisar 2015; Maley 2016). Fleming also played up his *bona fide* rebelliousness, stating in his declaration of candidacy that "I not only fought the liberals in Washington, I also fought the leadership of my own party when they were all too willing to compromise on our conservative principles." He too was endorsed by, or received donations from, conservative political groups like FreedomWorks and Club for Growth (Ballard 2016; Berry 2015). Unfortunately, he came in fifth place in the state's "jungle primary," winning just 11 percent of the vote.[71]

*Caucus size.* Finally, though the Freedom Caucus kept a cap on its membership, it also drew strength in numbers, so maintaining a sizeable number of

---

[69] Interview with Freedom Caucus member, March 6, 2018.

[70] This statistic should not be given too much weight, since it may be skewed by individual bills with large numbers of cosponsors, as well as by changes in the kinds of bills introduced from one Congress to another.

[71] Caucus member Mo Brooks (AL) ran for Senate in a special election in 2017 and came in third place with 20 percent of the vote, and in May 2018 Raúl Labrador lost the Idaho gubernatorial primary. A third Caucus member, Ron DeSantis, was elected governor of Florida later that year.

members was a key task of the bloc. While it was able to maintain its approximate size since it was formed in January 2015, the group also suffered from departures driven by dissatisfaction with its tactics, and its reputation as a collection of difficult troublemakers may help explain problems it had with recruitment.

In the 114th Congress, the Caucus lost several members who opted to retire or run for higher office, but more troubling were two high-profile exoduses attributable to the group's tactics and strategy. In mid-September 2015, amid a Caucus threat to hold government funding hostage in its effort to defund Planned Parenthood, Tom McClintock (CA) publicly left the group, upset by a confrontational legislative approach to bargaining that consistently "strip[ped] the House Republican majority of its ability to set the House agenda by combining with House Democrats on procedural motions" (Fuller 2015j).[72] Reid Ribble (NJ) followed in October, after Speaker Boehner announced his resignation, complaining that the Caucus had strayed from its mission by usurping the party's top leadership instead of focusing on policy.

The Freedom Caucus did manage to recruit more members to make up for these departures. Warren Davidson (OH), who won a 2016 special election to fill Speaker Boehner's seat and had been backed by the Freedom Caucus, immediately joined the group, and Joe Barton of Texas became a member late that year (Wegmann 2016a). But problems of retention attributable at least partly to the group's bargaining strategy continued in the 115th Congress, when two Republicans departed after the Caucus was assailed for blocking a major health care bill in 2017, and two others left as well (see section 6).[73] The group's record of success in recruiting new members after the 2016 election to make up for these and other departures[74] was also mixed. One likely recruit, Liz Cheney (WY), who had won the seat held by retiring Caucus member Cynthia Lummis, opted not to join; another freshmen member, Jim Banks (IN), whose campaign had benefited from House Freedom Fund advertising, also declined; and a freshman who had committed to joining the Caucus, Jason Lewis (MN), changed his mind. On the other hand, incumbent Republican Louie Gohmert

---

[72] In his resignation letter, McClintock cited several specific events related to his departure, including the DHS funding vote on February 27, the Caucus's positions on free trade in May, and its role in having an Iran disapproval resolution withdrawn.

[73] The other two Republicans, Barry Loudermilk (GA) and Keith Rothfus (PA), left in early 2017 (Hallerman 2017; Mauriello 2017).

[74] These included Mick Mulvaney (SC), who became Director of the Office of Management and Budget in the Trump Administration; Trent Franks (AZ), who resigned in early 2018 over allegations of sexual improprieties; and Jim Bridenstine (OK), who was confirmed as Director of NASA.

(TX) did join the group in early 2017, and three other freshmen who had been financially supported by the Freedom Fund did as well (Cahlink 2017; Collins 2017; Pathé 2017).

## 5.2 Conclusion

Though the Freedom Caucus had some legislative victories and helped push the incumbent Speaker from Congress, it serves as a cautionary example of the potential downsides to the use of threat-making. The group's members did worse in fundraising and vote share in the 2016 election cycle than their non-Caucus peers, burned bridges with their House colleagues, and failed to win higher elected office. The group itself remained largely unknown outside the Beltway, and while it stayed roughly the same size over time, it had some notable failures in member recruitment and retention.

In the next and final section, I review the findings of this study. I also discuss briefly how the Freedom Caucus's experience in the 115th Congress (2017–18), its first under unified Republican government, further illustrates the conditions that determine the likelihood of threat-making by a group of ideological extremists and underscores the pros and cons of hard bargaining in Congress.

## 6 Conclusion

Bargaining is a central feature of legislative politics. It can be beneficial, producing policy outcomes that are beneficial to the broader public. But it can also be detrimental, yielding positive outcomes for a bare majority (or even minority) of citizens, or it can simply fail altogether, resulting in political stalemate and an erosion of trust in and within the legislature. Much of the success and reputation of the U.S. Congress thus depends on the character of bargaining and negotiation among its members.

Using the House Freedom Caucus as a case study, this analysis has identified the costs and benefits of hard bargaining, and the use of threats in particular, within congressional parties. The unusual example of the Caucus shows that threat-making can block legislation, shift the legislative agenda, and even contribute to the premature departure of an incumbent party leader. However, threat-making is not costless, and those pursuing it must be prepared to weather substantial criticism and sanctions by party leaders and colleagues with few if any electoral gains.

In this section, I discuss briefly the ways that the Freedom Caucus's bargaining behavior changed and did not change after the 2016 elections, when it operated under a new, unified Republican governing regime. I also offer some final observations about what the Caucus has meant for the ideological direction of the House Republican Conference, the relationship between party leaders and the rank-and-file, and the future of threat-making and hard bargaining within Congress.

## 6.1 Threat-Making in a Changed Political Context

The election of Donald Trump as president in 2016 lessened several of the incentives for an ideologically extreme faction to oppose the legislative proposals of its party's leaders. With Republican control of the White House and majorities in Congress (albeit not a filibuster-proof majority in the Senate), GOP leaders could propose more-conservative legislation that had a realistic chance of becoming law. In addition, expectations to enact policy were greater, and the president could serve as an additional source of pressure on wayward lawmakers to cooperate. Trump also did unexpectedly well in many primary elections held in Freedom Caucus members' districts, suggesting the president could draw upon pro-Trump constituents in their districts to push the group in his direction, though he won most of their districts in the general election with a smaller margin than they did (Bacon 2017).

Freedom Caucus Republicans signaled a possible shift towards cooperation over confrontation early in the 115th Congress. The new chair of the bloc, Mark Meadows (R-NC), told reporters in January 2017 that "I think it's incumbent upon all of us to figure out how we can legislate going forward," including finding ways to cooperate with Trump and Speaker Ryan (Ferrechio 2017), and later that year he explained that "becoming so rigid in a unified government makes you miss opportunities" (Weaver 2017). At the same time, the group did not immediately curtail its overall objectives, and it saw no reason to expect its influence would decline. Both Meadows and former Caucus Chair Jim Jordan (R-OH) wrote in an editorial that their party had "no more excuses" not to repeal Obamacare, tighten the U.S.-Mexican border, or enact other conservative legislative proposals (Jordan and Meadows 2017). As one Caucus member told the author in early 2018, because the Republican Party was eager to enact legislation but lacked a majority on partisan matters without their votes, "our influence has certainly increased dramatically."[75] And the bloc realized it might be able to marshal more influence by building an alliance with powerful allies – another tactic it used in the 114th Congress, only this time, those allies could include President Trump and friendly White House staff like OMB Director and former Caucus member Mick Mulvaney (R-SC).

---

[75] Interview with Freedom Caucus member, March 6, 2018.

A brief review of Freedom Caucus activity during the first year of the 115th Congress suggests that the group was still confrontational, albeit less so than it had been in the past. The most illustrative example was the *attempted repeal and replacement of the Affordable Care Act.* The Caucus pushed for an early repeal of the act, and it endorsed a bill that would do mostly that (Weigel 2017). When Meadows objected to refundable tax credits included in a draft of the Republican leadership's own repeal bill, caps were added to the credits to restrain costs (Bade, Demko, and Haberkorn 2017). But Freedom Caucus members still criticized the bill as a rushed product written behind closed doors that created "a new entitlement program" via the tax credits, and a majority of them made a secret pledge to negotiate as a unit to change the measure and reject it if necessary (Bade 2017b; Bade, Dawsey, and Haberkorn 2017; Hellman 2017). Congressional leaders and the White House offered to make changes to the bill, but they were constrained by the need to keep Republican moderates on board and by the rules of the Senate, which permitted only moderate legislative changes lest the bill be subject to a filibuster (DeBonis 2017a). Despite these concessions, and heavy lobbying by GOP leaders and the White House, enough Freedom Caucus Republicans remained in opposition to the bill – joined by a handful of party moderates – to deny it a majority, and a scheduled vote on the measure was cancelled (Alberta 2017a; Bade, Dawsey, and Haberkorn 2017; Golshan 2017).

The Caucus faced a cavalcade of criticism from both the president and their colleagues for blocking a central agenda item of the party and shifting its demands during negotiations, and two of its members, Brian Babin and Ted Poe, abandoned the group (Bade, Dawsey, and Haberkorn 2017; Hilburn 2017; Nelson 2017). Caucus Chair Meadows then entered negotiations with the White House and Tom MacArthur (R-NJ), a leader of the Tuesday Group, a bloc of moderate Republicans. The result was a series of changes to the bill, endorsed by the Caucus, that would (among other things) allow states to exempt themselves from some requirements of the Affordable Care Act.[76] The group acknowledged that they were compromising their original demands, but maintained they were "keep[ing] our promise to the American people to lower healthcare costs," and conservative interest groups like FreedomWorks that had opposed the original bill stood behind the proposed changes (Cheney and Bade 2017; Meadows 2017). The amended bill narrowly passed the House, 217–213, and though the measure died in the Senate, Meadows believed the

---

[76] MacArthur subsequently resigned his post as co-chair of the Tuesday Group amid disgruntlement within the Group over his role negotiating the agreement (DeBonis 2017b).

Caucus had taken the best strategic path. "[H]ad there not been a bill that was pulled," he said, "there would always have been the idea that the Freedom Caucus will cave in the end ... [but] had we not come around ... there would have been the typical stereotype that they'll never get to 'yes'" (Weaver 2017).

On two other occasions, the Freedom Caucus withdrew threats to vote against a measure if certain conditions were unmet, primarily because the passage of another bill of major importance to the party was at stake. In January, Republican congressional leaders made the *passage of a budget resolution* their top priority, since it would allow the repeal of the Affordable Care Act by a simple majority in the Senate, avoiding a filibuster. The resolution would permit significant spending deficits, however, and some wary Caucus members sought to delay its passage until the exact method of repealing the health care law was determined. The group ultimately decided not to officially oppose the measure after receiving assurances from leadership that their concerns would be addressed, though Caucus Chair Meadows insisted the group could have defeated the bill had it wanted to (Bade 2017a; Fuller 2017a; Newhauser 2017; Snell and Weigel 2017). It passed on a largely party-line vote, with only two Caucus members voting no.

The group also ended up conceding its original demands during an effort to enact a *second budget resolution*. As with the first budget resolution, the second resolution needed to pass both chambers in order for the Senate to enact a bill of high priority to the GOP – this time, tax reform – by a simple majority vote. But efforts to draft a resolution in the Budget Committee hit a snag because the Caucus was "threatening to withhold its support ... unless deeper cuts are made to mandatory spending, largely in welfare programs," and GOP moderates in turn opposed any additional spending cuts (Bade and Ferris 2017; Elis 2017b). After the Senate passed its own budget resolution, with Republicans desperate to enact tax reform before the end of the calendar year, Meadows admitted "feeling the pressure to get this done" and thus "willing to negotiate a little bit more generously" (DeBonis 2017c). Despite the resolution's dramatic increase in the federal deficit, most of the Caucus voted with all but 20 other Republicans to narrowly pass the resolution in October, 216–212 (Taylor and Davis 2017).

These cases suggest that the changed political context had made it less appealing for the Freedom Caucus to employ hard bargaining.[77] Nonetheless,

---

[77] A shift in Caucus leadership may have also contributed to its change in bargaining strategy. One opinion writer argued that Meadows is "affable and outgoing" (Hunt 2018), and, according to a reporter, "many argue that Jordan was a better fit for the Obama years but Meadows is right for today" (Weaver 2017).

one should not conclude that the bloc was unwedded to conservative policy goals. Unified government meant that GOP leaders could propose more-conservative legislation knowing it had a realistic chance of being signed into law,[78] and though their initial Obamacare repeal bill was deemed insufficiently conservative by the Freedom Caucus, party leaders' bold tax-cutting bill was desirable enough to convince the group to withdraw its opposition to the second budget resolution. Even the Caucus's compromise Obamacare repeal language moved the legislation in a more rightward direction, such as by permitting states to be exempt from mandated coverage for emergency room and maternity care (Kaplan and Pear 2017).

Nor did the Freedom Caucus always surrender or compromise, and on at least two occasions it used threats to try to persuade GOP leaders to change direction. In May 2017, the group had officially opposed a "clean" *debt ceiling bill*, and it subsequently proposed language that could be added to the bill that would cut federal spending or otherwise reduce the debt (Elis 2017a; McCrimmon 2017). Before a final deal could be struck with GOP leaders, President Trump negotiated with Democrats to pass a rival bill that had none of the provisions sought for by the Caucus, and even included funding for disaster relief, a move opposed by congressional GOP leaders. Nonetheless, the bill passed in September by a wide margin, with over half the Caucus voting against it (Kaplan and Shear 2017; "September Starts Out as a Disastrous Month"). Two months later, when the House was about to consider funding the *Children's Health Insurance Program (CHIP)*, the Caucus threatened to defeat the rule for considering it when party leaders tried to use the rule to alter how the program would be paid for. GOP leaders subsequently backed down (Fuller 2017b).

## 6.2 The Future of Threat-Making and the Republican Party

What does the story of the Freedom Caucus tell us more broadly about the future of hard bargaining in Congressional negotiations and the future of the Republican Party in general? Many of the bigger forces that incentivize threat-making or discourage constructive bargaining across parties are unlikely to dissipate soon. Voters, fueled by partisan media and party activists, will probably continue to press their representatives in Congress to avoid compromise, and many issues will likely remain deeply divisive. It is telling that, while

---

[78] The procedural requirements of the Senate remained a problem, but the Caucus seems to have been cognizant of the need to comply with those requirements, which one would expect if the group preferred enacting policy over position-taking opportunities to blame Senate Democrats for filibustering desired bills.

lawmaking in general may be no more partisan than it was four decades ago (Curry and Lee 2017), most legislative initiatives examined in this study were characterized by little if any bargaining in the House between majority Republicans and minority Democrats – except when, ironically, threats by the Freedom Caucus brought the two parties together to enact must-pass bills.

What is less clear is whether hard-nosed bargaining *within* parties is as durable. The changing behavior of the Freedom Caucus suggests that the use of threats by an intraparty faction has its limits. Under conditions of unified party government, the group proved more vulnerable to political pressure to abandon threats against their own party's leaders and seek legislative compromises. Even in divided party government, threats within parties are neither inevitable nor always desirable. Recall how the Freedom Caucus acted strategically during its first two years, sometimes drawing upon support from allies to achieve its political or policy objectives instead of relying on threats alone. Furthermore, the group and its members did suffer some reputational, electoral, and other costs (or at least gained no additional benefits in those areas).

Much also depends on the future of both the Freedom Caucus and the Republican Party. In retrospect, the Caucus failed to move the GOP in a more conservative direction. It proved unable to enact substantial conservative legislation in the 114th Congress, and the GOP nominated an unorthodox former Democrat for the presidency who appeared to have few strong ideological preferences. However, the Caucus did serve as a bellwether of growing disdain by Republican voters for party elites, and some GOP congressional candidates emerged in 2018 who emulated Trump's style and campaign agenda (Oliphant 2018). If this disdain takes root, more Republicans may find strategic and electoral advantages in using hardball negotiation tactics against the party leaders whom the GOP's primary voters view with distrust.

In the short term, the future of intraparty bargaining also depends upon which political party controls the levers of power in the national government. As of this writing, the Caucus remains a robust organization. But Democrats have captured control of the House, so will the Freedom Caucus remain as vibrant a faction when it is nestled within a minority party as opposed to a majority party? Will its members maintain loyalty to an unpopular president whose attachment to conservative principles often appears tenuous at best? And could a Freedom Caucus–like group emerge within the Democratic Party, continuing the tradition of demanding policy concessions in exchange for its vote? The answers to these questions will be determined largely by the voting bases of both parties, which party controls Congress, the fate of the Trump presidency, and the kinds of lawmakers who are chosen to lead both congressional parties and the intraparty factions within them. With so many unknowns, it is impossible to predict with certainty whether legislative hardball of the kind practiced by the House Freedom Caucus will endure. But the example of the Caucus serves as a testament to the effectiveness and drawbacks of aggressive legislative bargaining.

# References

"Abortion Debate Heats Up Again as Foes Target Planned Parenthood." In *CQ Almanac* 2015, 71st ed. Washington D.C.: CQ-Roll Call.

Alberta, Tim (2016a). "Inside Trump's Conquest of America's Most Conservative Districts." *National Review*, August 15.

(2016b). "Conservatism in the Era of Trump." *National Review*, December 21.

(2017a). "Inside the GOP's Health Care Debacle." *Politico*, March 24.

(2017b). "John Boehner Unchained." *Politico Magazine*, November/ December.

(2018). "'This Is a Place That Just Sucks Your Soul.'" *Politico*, June 15.

Bacon, Perry Jr. (2017). "Should the Freedom Caucus Be Afraid of Donald Trump?" *FiveThirtyEight.com*, March 31. https://fivethirtyeight.com/fea tures/should-the-freedom-caucus-be-afraid-of-donald-trump/, accessed April 23, 2018.

Bade, Rachael (2016a). "Freedom Caucus Strong-Armed Ryan on IRS Impeachment." *Politico*, May 18.

(2016b). "House GOP Delays Gun Vote after Own Members Object." *Politico*, July 5.

(2016c). "The Other Speaker of the House." *Politico*, September 28.

(2016d). "Freedom Caucus Weighs Request to Delay Leadership Election." *Politico*, September 28.

(2016e). "Freedom Caucus Divided over Ryan Ouster." Politico, October 27.

(2017a). "Freedom Caucus Looks to Delay Budget – and Obamacare Repeal." *Politico*, January 9.

(2017b). "Conservatives Escalate Threats to Tank Obamacare Repeal." *Politico*, March 12.

Bade, Rachael and John Bresnahan (2016). "Freedom Caucus Will Oppose Ryan's 'Anti-Terror' Legislation." *Politico*, July 6.

Bade, Rachael and Heather Caygle (2016). "Freedom Caucus Stiffs GOP on Campaign Cash." *Politico*, September 20.

Bade, Rachel, Josh Dawsey, and Jennifer Haberkorn (2017). "How a Secret Freedom Caucus Pact Brought Down Obamacare Repeal." *Politico*, March 26.

Bade, Rachael, Paul Demko, and Jennifer Haberkorn (2017). "GOP Unveils Obamacare Replacement amid Sharp Party Divide." *Politico*, March 6.

Bade, Rachael and Sarah Ferris (2017). "Centrist Republicans Mobilize against Draft GOP Budget." *Politico*, June 29.

Bade, Rachael and Ben Weyl (2016). "House GOP Clashes over Plan to Avoid Government Shutdown." *Politico*, September 9.

Baer, Emily Caitlin (2017). "Organizing for Reform: The Democratic Study Group and the Role of Party Factions in Driving Institutional Change in the House of Representatives." Ph.D. dissertation, University of Minnesota.

Ballard, Mark (2016). "Conservative Group Backs John Fleming in Senate Race." *The Acadiana Advocate*, October 21. www.theadvocate.com/acadiana/news/politics/elections/article_d5b2e48a-97c4-11e6-b4f9-4f2a5c3596b5.html, accessed February 19, 2018.

Baron, David P. and John A. Ferejohn (1989). "Bargaining in Legislatures." *American Political Science Review* 83(4), 1181–1206.

Berman, Russell (2014). "Hensarling Calls for an End to the Export-Import Bank." *The Hill*, May 21.

Berry, Deborah Barfield (2015). "Rep. Fleming Officially Enters Louisiana Senate Race." *The Daily Advertiser*, December 7. www.theadvertiser.com/story/news/2015/12/07/rep-fleming-officially-enters-louisiana-senate-race/76941138/f, accessed February 19, 2018.

Bialik, Carl and Aaron Bycoffe (2015). "The Hard-Line Republicans Who Pushed John Boehner Out." *FiveThirtyEight.com*, September 25. https://fivethirtyeight.com/features/the-hard-line-republicans-who-pushed-john-boehner-out/, accessed March 13, 2018.

Binder, Sarah A. (2015). "This Is Why Some Republicans Keep Threatening to Take the Government Hostage." *The Monkey Cage, Washington Post*, September 16. www.washingtonpost.com/news/monkey-cage/wp/2015/09/16/this-is-why-some-republicans-keep-threatening-to-take-the-government-hostage/, accessed November 9, 2017.

Binder, Sarah A. and Frances E. Lee (2016). "Making Deals in Congress." From Jane Mansbridge and Cathie Jo Martin, eds., *Political Negotiation: A Handbook*. Washington, D.C.: Brookings Institution Press.

Black, Duncan. (1958). *The Theory of Committees and Elections*. Cambridge: Cambridge University Press.

Boatright, Robert G. (2014). "The 2014 Congressional Primaries in Context." Presented at What the 2014 Primaries Foretell About the Future of American Politics, Washington, D.C. www.cfinst.org/pdf/papers/Boatright_2014_Primaries_in_Context_9–30-14.pdf, accessed March 13, 2018.

Boland, Barbara (2015). "Meadows: Congress Must Stop Lurching from 'Crisis to Crisis.'" *The Washington Examiner*, October 7.

Bolton, Alexander (2015). "Boehner Seeks Final Budget Deal." *The Hill*, September 30.

Bolton, Alexander and Sarah Ferris (2015). "White House, GOP Strike Budget Deal." *The Hill*, October 27.

Bowman, Bridget (2015). "House Committee Approves Resolution Blocking D.C. Law." *Roll Call*, April 21.

Buck, Ken (2017). "Freedom Caucus Member Reveals GOP's 'Vindictive Retaliation'." *New York Post*, April 8. http://nypost.com/2017/04/08/freedom-caucus-member-exposes-gops-vindictive-retaliation/, accessed October 28, 2017.

Cahlink, George (2017). "Usually Fractious Freedom Caucus Works Quietly on Energy." *E&E News*, May 17. www.eenews.net/stories/1060054645, accessed March 13, 2018.

Cahn, Emily (2015). "Blum Says Others Will Support Him If Republicans Don't." *Roll Call*, June 12.

Carson, Jamie L., Michael H. Crespin, and Anthony J. Madonna (2014). "Procedural Signaling, Party Loyalty, and Traceability in the U.S. House of Representatives." *Political Research Quarterly* 67(4), 729–742.

Cheney, Kyle and Rachael Bade (2017). "Freedom Caucus Endorses Obamacare Repeal Compromise." *Politico*, April 26.

Cirilli, Kevin (2015). "Republican Study Committee Comes out Against Ex-Im." *The Hill*, May 21.

Clarke, Andrew J. (n.d.). "The House Freedom Caucus: Extreme Faction Influence in the U.S. Congress." Working Paper. www.andrewjclarke.net/uploads/2/8/0/2/28027431/freedomcaucus.pdf, accessed November 6, 2017.

(2017). "Trump Is Tweeting Threats at the Freedom Caucus. Good Luck with That." *Washington Post Monkey Cage*, April 5. www.washingtonpost.com/news/monkey-cage/wp/2017/04/05/trump-is-tweeting-threats-at-the-freedom-caucus-good-luck-with-that/, accessed May 1, 2018.

Clarke, Andrew J., Jeffery A. Jenkins, and Nathan W. Monroe (2016). "From Rolls to Disappointments: Examining the Other Sources of Majority Party Failure in Congress." *Political Research Quarterly* 70(1), 82–97.

Cogan, Marin (2015). "The Trade Vote Reignited the War Within the House GOP." *New York Magazine Daily Intelligencer*, June 26. http://nymag.com/daily/intelligencer/2015/06/house-gops-family-feud.html, accessed April 23, 2018.

Collins, Eliza (2017). "Two Marks, Meadows and Walker, Leave Mark on Obamacare Repeal Bill." *USA Today*, March 22.

"Congress Grants President Fast-Track Authority for Trade Deals." In *CQ Almanac* 2015, 71st ed. Washington D.C.: CQ-Roll Call.

Corombos, Greg (2015). "'Freedom Caucus' Vows to Keep GOP Promises.'" *WND.com*, January 28. www.wnd.com/2015/01/freedom-caucus-vows-to-keep-gop-promises/, accessed April 23, 2018.

Cottle, Michelle (2016a). "The House Freedom Caucus Is Trying to Be Reasonable." *The Atlantic*, May 12.

(2016b). "The Conservative Crusade Against the IRS Commissioner." *The Atlantic*, October 7.

Cox, Gary W. and Mathew D. McCubbins (1993). *Legislative Leviathan*. Berkeley: University of California Press.

(1994). "Bonding, Structure, and the Stability of Political Parties: Party Government in the House." *Legislative Studies Quarterly* 19(2), 215–231.

(2005). *Setting the Agenda: Responsible Party Government in the U.S. House of Representatives*. New York: Cambridge University Press.

Curry, James M. and Frances E. Lee (2017). "Non-Party Government: Bipartisan Lawmaking and Theories of Party Power in Congress." Paper presented at the 2017 Congress and History Conference, Washington, D.C.

Davis, Aaron C. (2015). "House Votes to Strike Down D.C. Law Banning Reproductive Discrimination." *Washington Post*, April 30.

DeBonis, Mike (2015a). "How Conservatives Are Keeping the Gay Marriage Issue Alive on Capitol Hill." *Washington Post*, July 17.

(2015b). "House Conservatives Spurn McCarthy, Flex Muscle Ahead of Speaker Vote." *Washington Post*, October 7.

(2015c). "Rep. Jim Jordan Will Remain House Freedom Caucus Chairman." *Washington Post*, November 16.

(2017a). "What the Freedom Caucus Wants in the GOP Health-Care Bill, and Why It's Not Getting It," *Washington Post*, March 22.

(2017b). "Health-Care Fallout Prompts Tom MacArthur to Resign as Co-chair of Centrist House GOP Caucus." *Washington Post*, May 23.

(2017c). "House Hard-liners to Back Senate's Deficit-Raising Budget." *Washington Post*, October 25.

DeBonis, Mike and Paul Kane (2015). "Boehner in Pinch on DHS Funding." *Washington Post*, March 2.

DeBonis, Mike and Katie Zezima (2015). "GOP's Populist Revolt Arrives at Capitol, Complicating Iran Debate." *Washington Post*, September 9.

Den Hartog, Chris and Timothy P. Nokken (2017). "Is the Tea Party Different?" Presented at the Midwest Political Science Association, Chicago, IL.

Dennis, Steven T. (2015). "Obama Won't Sign TPA Without TAA 'Path'." *Roll Call*, June 17.

DeSilver, Drew (2015a). "What Is the House Freedom Caucus, and Who's in It?" *Pew Research Center*, October 20. www.pewresearch.org/fact-tank/ 2015/10/20/house-freedom-caucus-what-is-it-and-whos-in-it/, accessed September 17, 2017.

(2015b). "Freedom Caucus Districts Look Much Like Other GOP-Held Districts." *Pew Research Center*, October 22. www.pewresearch.org/ fact-tank/2015/10/22/freedom-caucus-districts-look-much-like-other-gop-held-districts/, accessed October 22, 2015.

Disler, Matthew (2015). "House Young Guns Buck Boehner on Trade." *Real Clear Politics*, June 20. www.realclearpolitics.com/articles/2015/06/20/ house_young_guns_buck_boehner_on_trade.html, accessed March 22, 2018.

Dixit, Avinash K. and Barry J. Nalebuff (1991). *Thinking Strategically: The Competitive Edge in Business, Politics, and Everyday Life*. New York: W. W. Norton.

Douglas, William (2017). "Conservatives' 'power of no' stifles Republican agenda." *Charlotte Observer*, August 2.

Draper, Robert (2012). *Do Not Ask What Good We Do: Inside the U.S. House of Representatives*. New York: Free Press.

Dumain, Emma (2015a). "House GOP Fails to Advance 3-Week DHS Funding Bill." *Roll Call*, February 27.

(2015b). "Second Republican Resigns From House Freedom Caucus." *Roll Call*, October 8.

(2015c). "House Republicans OK Changes to Steering Panel." *Roll Call*, November 19.

(2016). "Among House Republicans, Jockeying to Lose on Iran." *CQ Weekly*, September 8.

(2017). "In Role Reversal, Mick Mulvaney Trying to Get Conservatives to Back GOP Establishment Health Bill." *The Post and Courier*, March 8.

Dumain, Emma and Matt Fuller (2015a). "Trade Rule Passes Despite Conservative Mutiny." *Roll Call*, June 11.

(2015b). "Conservatives Fume Over Leadership's Crackdown on Rebels." *Roll Call*, June 22.

(2015c). "GOP Rewrite of 'No Child' Passes on Second Try." *Roll Call*, July 8.

Eigen, Lewis D. and Jonathan P. Siegel (1993). *The Macmillan Dictionary of Political Quotations*. New York: Macmillan Publishing.

Elis, Niv (2017a). "Freedom Caucus Opposes Clean Debt Ceiling Increase." *The Hill*, May 24.

(2017b). "House Budget Plan Delayed Again over Welfare Cuts." *The Hill*, June 27.

Eno, Robert (2017). "Who's in the Freedom Caucus and Why Is It Important?" *Conservative Review*, April 4. www.conservativereview.com/commen tary/2017/04/whos-in-the-house-freedom-caucus-and-why-is-it-impor tant, accessed April 6, 2017.

Farrell, John A. (2001). *Tip O'Neill and the Democratic Century* Boston: Little, Brown.

Fenno, Richard F. Jr. (1973). *Congressmen in Committees*. Boston: Little, Brown.

Ferrechio, Susan (2015). "Conservatives Likely to Lose Education Reform Battle in Congress." *Washington Examiner*, July 8.

(2017). "Rep. Mark Meadows Will Preside over a More Cooperative Wing of Conservative Rebels." *Washington Examiner*, January 3.

Ferris, Sarah (2016a). "House Conservative Leaders Want to Break Spending Deal." *The Hill*, February 25.

(2016b). "House GOP Comes to Terms with Prospect of No Budget." *The Hill*, April 13.

Flores, Bill (2015). "Republican Study Committee Unveils FY 2016 Government Funding Proposal." Press release, September 15. https://flores.house.gov/ news/documentsingle.aspx?DocumentID=398680, accessed April 28, 2018.

Foley, Elise (2015). "Conservatives Take Credit for Delay On Border Bill." *Huffington Post*, January 27. www.huffingtonpost.com/2015/01/27/conser vatives-house-border-bill_n_6555934.html, accessed October 9, 2017.

Fram, Alan and Emily Swanson (2015). "AP-GfK Poll: GOP Voters Prefer Combative Tactics over Budget." *Seattle Times*, October 27.

Fram, Alan and Andrew Taylor (2015). "The Complex Fight GOP Leaders Face to Avoid Another Federal Shutdown." *Associated Press*, September 13.

French, Lauren (2015a). "Conservatives Demand Vote to Reject D.C. Abortion Law." *Politico*, April 29.

(2015b). "Conservatives Issue Demands for their Votes on Trade Deal." *Politico*, June 3.

(2015c). "Emboldened House Conservatives Angle for Power." *Politico*, July 13.

(2015d). "Boehner Coup Leader an Army of One." *Politico*, July 29.

(2015e). "Freedom Caucus Giving Ryan Benefit of the Doubt." *Politico*, November 3.

(2016). "House Freedom Caucus to Break with Leadership on Budget." *Politico*, March 14.

French, Lauren and Seung Min Kim (2015). "Why the 'Hell No' Caucus Is Saying 'Yes' to the Budget." *Politico*, March 25.

French, Lauren and Anna Palmer (2015a). "DeSantis, Duncan Quit House Whip Team." *Politico*, February 5.

(2015b). "House Freedom Caucus Endorses Daniel Webster for Speaker." *Politico*, October 7.

French, Lauren and Jake Sherman (2015). "House GOP Leaders Take on Subcommittee Rebels." *Politico*, February 12.

Friedman, Dan (2016). "For These House Republicans, the NRA's Seal of Approval Isn't Enough." *The Trace*, July 13. www.thetrace.org/2016/07/freedom-caucus-house-conservatives-oppose-nra-backed-gun-bill/, accessed February 7, 2018.

Froman, Lewis A. Jr. and Randall B. Ripley (1965). "Conditions for Party Leadership: The Case of the House Democrats." *American Political Science Review* 59(1), 52–63.

"Frustrated with 'No Child Left Behind,' Congress Takes a New Path on Schools." In *CQ Almanac* 2015, 71st ed. Washington D.C.: CQ Roll Call.

Fuller, Matt (2014). "RSC Chairmanship Race Tests Conservatives." *Roll Call*, November 18.

(2015a). "House Freedom Caucus Looks to Be a Force – in Leadership and Lawmaking." *Roll Call*, February 4.

(2015b). "House Freedom Caucus Lines Up Opposition to Export-Import Bank." *Roll Call*, May 19.

(2015c). "Rule Vote Retribution Continues; Chaffetz Takes Away Subcommittee Gavel." *Roll Call*, June 20.

(2015d). "House Conservatives Emboldened, Despite Crackdown Attempt." *Roll Call*, July 6.

(2015e). "Quieter RSC Still Conservative, Still Effective, Chairman Says." *Roll Call*, July 14.

(2015f). "Freedom Caucus Forms 'Fight Club' in House." *Roll Call*, July 22.

(2015g). "Freedom Caucus to Leadership: Delay Iran Vote." *Roll Call*, September 8.

(2015h). "Conservatives Force Boehner to Rethink Iran." *Roll Call*, September 9.

(2015i). "Freedom Caucus to Oppose Any Spending Bill With Planned Parenthood Money." *Roll Call*, September 10.

(2015j). "House Freedom Caucus Loses Members Over Planned Parenthood." *Roll Call*, September 16.

(2015k). "HFC Looks for Leverage in Speaker's Race." *Roll Call*, October 7.

(2015l). "How the House Freedom Caucus Got Behind Paul Ryan." *Roll Call*, October 23.

(2015m). "Jim Jordan and the (Not So) Subtle Influence of the House Freedom Caucus." *Huffington Post*, November 19. www.huffingtonpost .com/entry/jim-jordan-house-freedom-caucus_us_564e1415e4b031745cf 04f1f, accessed April 19, 2018.

(2016a). "Paul Ryan Hosts Budget Meeting With House Freedom Caucus. It Didn't Go Well." *Huffington Post*, February 3. www.huffingtonpost.com/ entry/paul-ryan-budget-freedom-caucus_us_56b17510e4b01d80b244871a.

(2016b). "Paul Ryan Has a House Freedom Caucus Problem." *Huffington Post*, July 6. www.huffingtonpost.com/entry/paul-ryan-house-freedom-caucus_us_577d1b38e4b09b4c43c1bf55, accessed July 7, 2016.

(2017a). "Obamacare Repeal Could Be More Difficult Than House Republicans Think." *The Huffington Post*, January 12. www.huffington post.com/entry/obamacare-repeal-house-republicans_us_5876cd9de4 b092a6cae5424c, accessed May 1, 2018.

(2017b). "House Passes Children's Health Insurance Bill, But Kids Are No Closer to Health Insurance." *Huffington Post*, November 3. www.huffing tonpost.com/entry/house-chip-no-closer-political-games_us_59fc8b8 be4b0b0c7fa39c75b, accessed May 1, 2018.

Gehrke, Joel (2015a). "Meet the Freedom Caucus." *National Review*, January 26. www.nationalreview.com/article/412775/meet-freedom-caucus-joel-gehrke, accessed December 12, 2016.

(2015b). "Jim Jordan Puts GOP Leadership on Notice." *The Corner (Blog), National Review*, June 17. www.nationalreview.com/article/419875/jim-jordan-puts-gop-leadership-notice-joel-gehrke, accessed October 7, 2017.

Gerring, John (2006). *Case Study Research: Principles and Practices*. New York: Cambridge University Press.

Glaser, James M. and Jeffrey M. Berry (2018). "Compromising Positions: Why Republican Partisans Are More Rigid than Democrats." *Political Science Quarterly* 133(1), 99–125.

Golshan, Tara (2017). "Freedom Caucus Leader says Paul Ryan Still Doesn't Have the Votes for Health Bill, Even with the Amendments." *Vox*, March 20. www.vox.com/policy-and-politics/2017/3/20/14988906/freedom-cau cus-paul-ryan-amendments, accessed April 30, 2018.

Gramlich, John (2017). "Many Americans Haven't Heard of the House Freedom Caucus." *Pew Research Center*, April 18. www.pewresearch .org/fact-tank/2017/04/18/many-americans-havent-heard-of-the-house-freedom-caucus/, accessed April 22, 2018.

Green, Matthew N. (2002). "Institutional Change, Party Discipline, and the House Democratic Caucus, 1911–1919." *Legislative Studies Quarterly* 27, 601–633.

——— (2016). "The Multiple Roots of Party Loyalty: Explaining Republican Dissent in the U.S. House of Representatives." *Congress and the Presidency* 43(1), 103–123.

Green, Matthew N. and Briana Bee (2016). "Keeping the Team Together: Explaining Party Discipline and Dissent in the U.S. Congress." In *Party and Procedure in the United States Congress*, ed. Jacob Straus and Matt Glassman, 41–62. Lanham, MD: Rowman & Littlefield.

Green, Matthew N. and Douglas B. Harris (2019). *Choosing the Leader: Leadership Elections in the U.S. House of Representatives*. New Haven: Yale University Press.

Grossman, Matt and David A. Hopkins (2016). *Asymmetric Politics: Ideological Republicans and Group Interest Democrats*. New York: Oxford University Press.

Haberkorn, Jennifer (2015). "18 GOP Members Draw Line in Planned Parenthood Fight." *Politico*, July 29.

Hallerman, Tamar (2017). "Barry Loudermilk Quietly Leaves the House Freedom Caucus." *Atlanta Journal-Constitution Political Insider* (blog), March 2. https://politics.myajc.com/blog/politics/barry-loudermilk-quietly-leaves-the-house-freedom-caucus/WFJ2dkEShsrj8RAaeCod7L/, accessed April 23, 2018.

Hammond, Susan Webb (1998). *Congressional Caucuses in National Policy Making*. Baltimore: Johns Hopkins University Press.

Hammond, Thomas H. and Gary J. Miller (1987). "Distant Friends and Nearby Enemies: The Politics of Legislative Coalition Formation." *Public Choice* 53(3), 277–284.

Hawkings, David (2015). "After the Revolution, a Single New Spot of Influence for the Freedom Caucus." *Roll Call*, December 14.

Hellman, Jesse (2017). "Freedom Caucus members say GOP doesn't have votes to pass healthcare plan." *The Hill*, March 7.

Herszenhorn, David M. (2015). "Hard-Line Republicans Want to Change More Than House Speaker." *New York Times*, October 7.

Hilburn, Greg (2017). "Abraham, Higgins: Blame GOP Freedom Caucus for Saving Obamacare." *USA Today*, March 25.

Ho, Catherine and Kelsey Snell (2015). "Export-Import Bank Supporters Move to Force House Vote." *Washington Post*, October 12.

"Homeland Bill Takes a Two-Step." In *CQ Almanac* 2015, 71st ed. Washington D.C.: CQ Roll Call.

House, Billy (2016). "Ryan Tames Conservative House Republicans Who Tormented Boehner." *Bloomberg Politics*, September 16.

"House Border Bill Pleases Neither Party." In *CQ Almanac* 2015, 71st ed. Washington D.C.: CQ Roll Call.

"House Freedom Caucus Helps Define Tense Power Dynamic in Congress." In *CQ Almanac* 2016, 72nd ed. Washington D.C.: CQ Roll Call.

Howell, Tom Jr. (2015). "Peter King: Freedom Caucus Wants to 'Hijack the Party and Blackmail the House.'" *Washington Times*, October 8.

Huetteman, Emmarie (2016). "Stopgap Bill Is Approved, Avoiding a Shutdown." *New York Times*, September 29.

Hunt, Albert R. (2018). "Freedom Caucus in Spotlight as Shutdown Looms." *Bloomberg*, January 14. www.bloomberg.com/view/articles/2018–01-14/freedom-caucus-in-spotlight-as-shutdown-looms, accessed April 24, 2018.

Jagoda, Naomi (2016). "House Rejects GOP Rep's Push for Vote on Impeaching IRS Head." *The Hill*, December 6.

Jenkins, Jeffery A. and Nathan W. Monroe (2015). "On Measuring Legislative Agenda-Setting Power." *American Journal of Political Science* 60(1): 158–174.

Jenkins, Jeffery A. and Charles Stewart III (2013). *Fighting for the Speakership: The House and the Rise of Party Government*. Princeton, NJ: Princeton University Press.

Jones, Jeffrey M. (2015). "Boehner Image Slightly Better After Resignation Announcement." *Gallup*, October 15.

Jordan, Jim (2015). "Mission Statement." Facebook post, January 26. www.facebook.com/repjimjordan/posts/10152998342301460, accessed April 18, 2018.

Jordan, Jim and Mark Meadows (2017). "No More Excuses, Republicans." *The Hill*, January 11.

Kamisar, Ben (2015). "Tea Party Candidates to Skip Senate Incumbent Challenges." *The Hill*, November 10.

Kane, Paul (2015). "House Votes to Renew Ex-Im Bank." *Washington Post*, October 28.

Kane, Paul and David A. Fahrenthold (2013). "Boehner's Laid-Back Approach Seen as Boon, Bane for House Republicans." *Washington Post*, June 29.

Kane, Paul and Kelsey Snell (2015). "GOP Tries to Avert Shutdown as Right Spoils for Planned Parenthood Fight." *Washington Post*, September 9.

Kaplan, Thomas and Robert Pear (2017). "House Passes Measure to Repeal and Replace the Affordable Care Act." *New York Times*, May 4.

Kaplan, Thomas and Michael D. Shear (2017). "House Passes Hurricane Aid and Raises Debt Ceiling." *New York Times*, September 8.

Karol, David (2009). *Party Position Change in American Politics: Coalition Management*. New York: Cambridge University Press.

King, Robert (2017). "Freedom Caucus Leader Mark Meadows: I Promised Full Obamacare Repeal." Washington Examiner, March 24.

Kofmehl, Kenneth (1964). "Institutionalization of a Voting Bloc." *Western Political Quarterly* 17(2), 256–272.

Krehbiel, Keith (1998). *Pivotal Politics: A Theory of U.S. Lawmaking*. Chicago: University of Chicago Press.

Kull, Steven and Nancy Gallagher (2015). "Assessing the Iran Deal: A Survey of the National Citizens Cabinet." Program for Public Consultation, School of Public Policy, University of Maryland.

"Labor Bloc Maps Wage Bill Revolt" (1937). *New York Times*, November 19.

Laslo, Matt (2016). 'Tea Party Cuts Off GOP Terror Bill to Spite Democrats." *The Daily Beast*, July 7. www.thedailybeast.com/tea-party-cuts-off-gop-terror-bill-to-spite-democrats, accessed March 2, 2018.

Lizza, Ryan (2015). "A House Divided." *New Yorker*, December 14.

Lochhead, Carolyn (2015). "Nancy Pelosi's Leadership Style Helps Her Avoid Crises Like GOP's." *San Francisco Chronicle*, October 16.

McCrimmon, Ryan (2017). "House Freedom Caucus to Air Debt Ceiling Demands." *Roll Call*, July 20.

McGee, Zachary A. (2017). "Keeping Your Friends Close: A Study of Punishment and Intraparty Insurgency." Paper presented at the Annual Meeting of the Midwest Political Science Association, Chicago, IL.

McPherson, Lindsey (2015). "These Eight Republicans Could Save the Conference from Breaking." *Roll Call*, November 18.

(2016). "House Conservatives Refuse Compromise with Ryan on Budget." *Roll Call*, March 3.

Maley, Mark (2016). "Todd Young beats Marlin Stutzman in GOP primary for US Senate seat." *The Elkhart Truth*, May 4.

Mann, Thomas E. and Norman J. Ornstein (2012). *It's Even Worse Than It Looks: How the American Constitutional System Collided with the New Politics of Extremism*. New York: Basic Books.

Marcos, Cristina (2017). "Jordan Won't Run for Oversight Gavel." *The Hill*, May 23.

Mauriello, Tracie (2017). "Freedom Caucus May Play Role in Alternate Obamacare Repeal Timeline." *Pittsburgh Post-Gazette*, January 6.

Mayhew, David R. (1974). *Congress: The Electoral Connection*. New Haven: Yale University Press.

(2005). *Divided We Govern: Party Control, Lawmaking, and Investigations, 1946–2002*. 2nd ed. New Haven: Yale University Press.

Meadows, Jon (2017). "FreedomWorks Urges House to Adopt MacArthur-Meadows Amendment to AHCA." Press release, FreedomWorks, April 26. www.freedomworks.org/content/freedomworks-urges-house-adopt-macarthur-meadows-amendment-ahca, accessed July 26, 2018.

Meadows, Mark (2015). "Conservatives Form House Freedom Caucus." Press release, January 26. https://meadows.house.gov/news/documentsingle .aspx?DocumentID=367, accessed April 18, 2018.

Meyer, Dick (2015). "Maybe the 'Crazies' in the House GOP Really Are Crazy." *York Dispatch*, October 5.

Nelson, Louis (2017). "Rep. Poe Explains Why He Split from the House Freedom Caucus." *Politico*, March 27.

Newell, Jim (2015). "The Freedom Caucus Is Nothing but Cowards." *Slate*, October 26. www.slate.com/articles/news_and_politics/politics/2015/10/ freedom_caucus_frightened_by_criticism_for_allowing_paul_ryan_ s_house_speaker.html, accessed February 19, 2018.

Newhauser, Daniel (2014). "As Flores Wins RSC Race, Tension Simmers Between Leaders and Conservatives." *The Atlantic*, November 18.

(2017). "Freedom Caucus Won't Block Obamacare Repeal Plan." *National Journal*, January 11.

Newton-Small, Jay (2015). "House Conservatives Brace for GOP Blowback in Leadership Fight." *Time*, October 19. http://time.com/4078961/house-repub licans-congress-leadership-fight-freedom-caucus/, accessed February 27, 2018.

North, Douglass C. and Barry R. Weingast (1989). "Constitutions and Commitment: The Evolution of Institutions Governing Public Choice in Seventeenth-Century England." *The Journal of Economic History* 49(4), 803–832.

Oliphant, James (2018). "'Mini-Trump' Candidates Battle It out in Republican Primaries." Reuters, May 6.

Ota, Alan K. (2016). "Freedom Caucus Moves to Force Vote on Impeaching IRS Chief." *Roll Call*, September 13.

Palmer, Doug and Adam Behsudi (2015). "Froman, Liberal Democrats Clash on Trade Authority." *Politico*, January 21.

Pathé, Simone (2017). "Freshmen Backed by Freedom Caucus Aren't Committing to Joining." *Roll Call*, January 11.

Paulsen, George Edward (1959). "The Legislative History of the Fair Labor Standards Act." Ph.D. dissertation, The Ohio State University.

Pearson, Kathryn (2015). *Party Discipline in the U.S. House of Representatives.* Ann Arbor, MI: University of Michigan Press.

Pew Research Center (2014). "Political Polarization in the American Public." June 12. www.people-press.org/2014/06/12/section-4-political-compro mise-and-divisive-policy-debates/, accessed April 3, 2018.

Raju, Manu (2015). "How the White House Kept Democrats from Killing the Iran Deal." *CNN*, September 11.

Reeve, Elspeth (2013). "The Secret iPad List to Bring Down Boehner." *The Wire*, January 4. http://www.thewire.com/politics/2013/01/secret-ipad-list-bring-down-boehner/60592/, accessed October 21, 2015.

Rein, Lisa (2015). "House GOP Moves to Impeach IRS Chief." *Washington Post*, October 28.

"Rep. Boehner: House Has 'Done Its Job' On Homeland Security Funding" (2015). Plus Media Solutions, February 26.

Reynolds, Molly E. and Richard L. Hall (2019). "Financing the 2016 Congressional Elections." In *Financing the 2016 Elections*, David B. Magleby, ed. Washington, D.C.: Brookings Institution Press.

Richman, Jesse (2011). "Parties, Pivots, and Policy: The Status Quo Test." *American Political Science Review* 105(1), 151–165.

Rubin, Ruth Bloch (2017). *Building the Bloc: Intraparty Organization in the U. S. Congress*. New York: Cambridge University Press.

Savransky, Rebecca (2017). "Poe: Some Freedom Caucus Members Would Vote Against Ten Commandments." *The Hill*, March 27.

Schelling, Thomas C. (1960). *The Strategy of Conflict*. Cambridge, MA: Harvard University Press.

  (2006). *Strategies of Commitment and Other Essays*. Cambridge, MA: Harvard University Press.

Schickler, Eric and Greg Wawro (2006). *Filibuster: Obstruction and Lawmaking in the U.S. Senate*. Princeton: Princeton University Press.

"September Starts Out as a Disastrous Month" (2017). *Congressional Quarterly Weekly Report*, September 11.

Severns, Maggie (2015). "House Republicans Put off No Child Left Behind Vote." *Politico*, February 27.

Shabad, Rebecca (2015). "28 Republicans Pledge to Oppose Any Bill Funding Planned Parenthood." *The Hill*, September 8.

Shepsle, Kenneth A. (1991). "Discretion, Institutions, and the Problem of Government Commitment." From Pierre Bourdieu and James S. Coleman, eds., *Social Theory for a Changing Society*. Boulder, CO: Westview Press.

Sherman, Jake (2015). "Rep. Jones Calls for Candidates with 'Misdeeds' to Withdraw from Leadership Race." *Politico*, October 7.

Sherman, Jake and John Bresnahan (2015a). "Boehner Takes Revenge." *Politico*, January 6.

(2015b). "GOP Probably Stuck with Weakened Boehner." *Politico*, March 3.

Sherman, Jake and Lauren French (2015). "How Ryan Conquered the Freedom Caucus." *Politico*, October 22.

Sherman, Jake, Lauren French, and Anna Palmer (2015). "How Old-Fashioned Logrolling Produced Congress' Massive Budget Deal." *Politico*, December 18.

Sherman, Jake and Anna Palmer (2015a). "Behind John Boehner's Crackdown on Conservatives." *Politico*, June 24.

(2015b). "GOP Group That Hit Conservatives Changes Its Tune." *Politico*, December 8.

Siddiqui, Sabrina, Ben Jacobs, and Tom McCarthy (2015). "House Speaker John Boehner to Resign After Battle with Conservatives." *The Guardian*, September 25.

Siegel, Josh (2015). "Home in North Carolina, Mark Meadows Reflects on Move to Oust John Boehner With 'No Regrets'." *The Daily Signal*, August 24.

Smith, Steven S. (2007). *Party Influence in Congress*. New York: Cambridge University Press.

Snell, Kelsey (2015). "Conservative Holdouts Won't Budge on Trade Vote." *Washington Post*, June 10.

(2016). "Inside Ryan's Charm Campaign with the House Freedom Caucus." *Washington Post*, November 6.

Snell, Kelsey and David Weigel (2017). "Hard-Line Republicans Signal Reversal." *Washington Post*, January 6.

Strong, Jonathan (2013). "Speak Softly or Carry a Big Stick." *Congressional Quarterly Weekly Report*, January 14.

Sullivan, Peter (2015a). "No Planned Parenthood Cuts in GOP Funding Bill." *The Hill*, December 2.

(2015b). "Planned Parenthood Unscathed in Spending Bill." *The Hill*, December 16.

Sullivan, Sean (2015a). "House Passes Bill Fully Funding the Department of Homeland Security." *Washington Post*, March 3.

(2015b). "Insurgent Bloc of House Conservatives Proving to Be a Thorn in Boehner's Side." *Washington Post*, March 4.

Taylor, Jessica and Susan Davis (2017). "Congress Paves Way for Tax Legislation by Passing Budget Resolution." *National Public Radio*, October 26. www.npr.org/2017/10/26/560215916/congress-paves-way-for-tax-legislation-by-passing-budget-resolution, accessed April 24, 2018.

Theriault, Sean (2013). *The Gingrich Senators: The Roots of Partisan Warfare in Congress*. New York: Oxford University Press.

Travis, Shannon (2011). "Who Is the Tea Party Caucus in the House?" *CNN*, July 29. http://politicalticker.blogs.cnn.com/2011/07/29/who-is-the-tea-party-caucus-in-the-house/, accessed March 2, 2018.

"Unable to Block Nuclear Deal with Iran, Congress Gives Itself Review Authority." In *CQ Almanac* 2015, 71st ed. Washington D.C.: CQ Roll Call.

"U.S. Rep. Mark Meadows Sends Letter to Boehner, Cantor Encouraging House Leadership to Defund Obamacare." (2013). *HCPress.com*, August 22. www.hcpress.com/politics/u-s-rep-mark-meadows-sends-let ter-to-boehner-cantor-encouraging-house-leadership-to-defund-obama care.html, accessed April 19, 2018.

Volden, Craig and Alan E. Wiseman (2014). *Legislative Effectiveness in the United States Congress*. New York: Cambridge University Press.

Voteview (2015). "House: Vote on Clean DHS Funding Bill." Voteview blog, March 6. http://voteview.com/blog/?p=1233, accessed May 3, 2018.

Wallner, James (2015). "The Problem of Credible Commitment in Congressional Budgeting." *The Journal of Policy History* 27(2), 382–403.

Warmbrodt, Zachary, Jake Sherman, and Victoria Guida (2015). "Boehner and Hensarling Square off over Ex-Im Bank." *Politico*, April 30.

Weaver, Al (2017). "Freedom Caucus Chairman Mark Meadows Takes a Seat at the Top Table." *Washington Examiner*, July 24.

Wegmann, Philip (2016a). "Meet Warren Davidson, the Man Who Took John Boehner's Seat." *The Daily Signal*, June 14. http://dailysignal.com//print? post_id=270520, accessed June 16, 2016.

(2016b). "Why Freedom Caucus Cut Deal With GOP Leadership Cancelling Vote to Impeach IRS Chief." *The Daily Signal*, September 15. https:// stream.org/freedom-caucus-cut-deal-gop-leadership-canceling-vote-impeach-irs-chief/, accessed April 20, 2018.

Wehrman, Jessica (2015). "Boehner: Some in GOP Caucus 'Unrealistic.'" *Dayton Daily News*, September 28.

Weigel, David (2017). "Freedom Caucus Backs ACA 'Repeal and Replace' That Counts on Private Health Care." *Washington Post PowerPost*, February 15. www.washingtonpost.com/news/powerpost/wp/2017/02/ 15/freedom-caucus-ready-for-obamacare-replacement-that-expands-hcas-bans-abortion-funding/, accessed April 30, 2018.

Will, George (2017). "The Heartening Mission of the Freedom Caucus." *Washington Post*, April 13.

Wong, Scott (2015a). "Will Boehner Risk the Tea Party's Wrath?" *The Hill*, February 25.

(2015b). "New House Conservative Caucus Divided in Budget Vote." *The Hill*, March 26.

(2015c). "Ire from House Conservatives Puts Education Bill in Jeopardy." *The Hill*, April 23.

(2015d). "Punished GOP Lawmaker Stirs New Talk of Boehner Rebellion." *The Hill*, June 22.

(2015e). "House Could Vote on Highway Bill This Week." *The Hill*, July 13.

(2015f). "Leadership Allies Reject Effort to Move Funding Bill the Right." *The Hill*, December 16.

(2016). "Ryan Faces New Pressures from House Conservatives." *The Hill*, September 8.

Wong, Scott and Sylvan Lane (2016). "Ryan Secures Big Win with Bipartisan Puerto Rico Bill." *The Hill*, May 24.

Zeller, Shawn (2017). "Survey: Republicans See Harm from Freedom Caucus." *Roll Call*, May 4.

# Acknowledgments

The author gratefully acknowledges the suggestions and comments of Emily Baer, David Balducchi, David Barker, William Bendix, Sarah Binder, Matthew Glassman, John Haskell, Danny Hayes, Jennifer Lawless, Eric Lawrence, Frances Lee, Bryan Marshall, Ethan Porter, Molly Reynolds, Colleen Shogan, John Sides, Richard Skinner, Elizabeth Suhay, Michele Swers, Philip Wallach, James Wallner, Daniel Wirls, and Julie Wronski. He also thanks his anonymous interviewees, Eric Schreiber for his valuable research assistance, and his family for their love and patience.

Cambridge Elements ⹀

# American Politics

## Frances E. Lee
*University of Maryland-College Park*

Frances E. Lee is Professor of Government and Politics at the University of Maryland-College Park. She is author of *Insecure Majorities: Congress and the Perpetual Campaign* (2016), *Beyond Ideology: Politics, Principles and Partisanship in the U.S. Senate* (2009), and coauthor of *Sizing Up the Senate: The Unequal Consequences of Equal Representation* (1999).

## Advisory Board

Marc Hetherington *University of North Carolina at Chapel Hill*
Geoffrey C. Layman *University of Notre Dame*
Suzanne Mettler *Cornell University*
Hans Noel *Georgetown University*
Eric Schickler *University of California, Berkeley*
John Sides *George Washington University*
Laura Stoker *University of California, Berkeley*

## About the Series

American Politics publishes authoritative contributions on American politics. Emphasizing works that address big, topical questions within the American political landscape, the series is open to all branches of the subfield and actively welcomes works that bridge subject domains. It publishes both original new research on topics likely to be of interest to a broad audience and state-of-the-art synthesis and reconsideration pieces that address salient questions and incorporate new data and cases to inform arguments.

# Cambridge Elements ☰

# American Politics

## Elements in the Series

A full series listing is available at: www.cambridge.org/core/series/elements-in-american-politics

Printed in the United States
By Bookmasters